**Murdock Learning Resource
Center
George Fox College**
Newberg, Oregon 97132

DEMCO

Capitalism in Amsterdam in the 17th Century

Capitalism in Amsterdam in the 17th Century

BY VIOLET BARBOUR

Ann Arbor Paperbacks
THE UNIVERSITY OF MICHIGAN PRESS

PREFACE

This study when first contemplated was to have been a chapter in a book on Anglo-Dutch commercial rivalry in the seventeenth century. But the book remains stubbornly unfinished, while the chapter has taken on independent existence and is here presented. I welcome the opportunity it affords to express my thanks to the John Simon Guggenheim Foundation for a research fellowship, to the Social Science Research Council for a grant in aid, and to Vassar College for leaves on generous terms. Without this assistance the long delightful periods of study in Dutch and English archives and libraries could not have been. The courtesies and privileges enjoyed in the Gemeente Oud-Archief in Amsterdam, the Rijks Archief and the Koninklijcke Bibliotheek in the Hague, the Public Record Office, the London Library, and the British Museum in London, the Bodleian Library in Oxford, and the wise kindliness of their respective staffs, are gratefully remembered. I am indebted beyond accounting to Mr. Simon Hart, archivist in the Gemeente Oud-Archief, not only for guidance in using the massive resources of Amsterdam's archives, but also for generous encouragement, for valuable bibliographical advice, and for specific information some of which, with his permission, I have used in this study as the notes attest. In a more general but very real way I am indebted to Dr. J. G. van Dillen, distinguished Professor of Economic History in the University of Utrecht, for many helpful suggestions from the store of his knowledge of Amsterdam's history in her greatest period.

Here at home the librarians of the Vassar College Library have been untiring in their response to appeals for assistance. I would especially thank Miss Elizabeth Richards, Reference Librarian, who has been invincible in answering hard bibliographical questions; and Miss Rosalie Tucker for finding and borrowing through inter-library loan rare works needed for consultation. My colleague, Professor Evalyn Clark of the Department of History of Vassar College, spared time from

PREFACE

her own researches to procure photostats of some elusive material.

The first version of this study was read and helpfully criticized by Mr. Hart in Amsterdam, and by Professor Margaret Myers of the Department of Economics, of Vassar College, but in reworking the manuscript I have had ample opportunity to commit further errors for which they are in no way responsible. In the revision I have had the benefit of advice from Professor Sidney Painter of the Department of History of Johns Hopkins University.

VIOLET BARBOUR

Vassar College

CONTENTS

CONTENTS

CHAPTER I

RISE OF THE AMSTERDAM MARKET

Mediaeval capitalism, precocious and adventurous as it was, was sporadic in incidence. Its progress was hampered by forms of wealth difficult to negotiate. Markets were small, and the spirit which dominated them was local and exclusive. Industry shared this localism of outlook; it was generally decentralized in organization, and its tools and techniques, however, serviceable in the hands of skilled craftsmen, could not meet the demands of an enlarged market. Travel, whether by land or sea, was beset by dangers; means of transport were inadequate. There was an insufficiency of good coin and a relative abundance of bad. Inelasticity of credit was the product of these difficulties.

In the sixteenth and seventeenth centuries these conditions were yielding to change. Geographically early modern capitalism extended its radius, especially in the penetration of northern and eastern Europe, and in beginning the exploitation of other continents to which the age of discovery had opened seaways. In western Europe trade was slowly shifting from its ancient seats commanding the Mediterranean highway, to northern and western ports facing the North Sea or the Atlantic Ocean. Political consolidation in several European states opened new opportunities for profit-making to monied men in the financing of courts, administrative machinery, armaments, and war. This consolidation tended to widen and link home markets, and to stimulate competition for European and overseas trade. New supplies of the monetary metals provided an exchange medium sufficient to the dimensions of trade, and gave to capital a mobility not hitherto enjoyed. Communication between business centers was quickened, and striking advances in mining, industry, and transportation speeded the production and distribution of goods.

However controversial the economic results of the Reformation, it is indubitable that certain communities—Amsterdam among them as we shall see—profited by the dissemination

11

of skills and techniques brought in by exiles fleeing religious persecution, war, or war taxation. And under a regime of discrimination such as that to which Huguenots were subjected in France, nonconformists in England, and Jews almost everywhere, the exclusion of the heterodox or the unbelievers from opportunities in other fields of eminence resulted in a striking channeling of their energies in business. In such circumstances the unity of the religious group was apt to assume business as well as spiritual and social validity, and from this solidarity useful commercial and financial connections sometimes developed.

For the most part the new wine was sedulously poured into old bottles, those being the only bottles at hand. The student of the period becomes used to being surprised, if the bull may be pardoned, at the mediaevalism of the façade behind which a modern economy was taking shape. Manor, gild, and fair might be in process of dessication as economic institutions, but in law, and in the minds and habits of men, they were apt to display astonishing powers of survival. Burgher right, staple right, market right, local mint, and local toll persisted stubbornly in defiance of an expanding geography of trade. Even such hoary nuisances to the business world as strand law, *droit d'aubaine,* and sanctuary, made ghostly reappearances even in the late seventeenth century. The most modern features of the economic life of this period—the metropolitan entrepôt in which a large part of European trade was concentrated, the bourse or commodity exchange, and the joint-stock company by which large commercial and industrial enterprises were financed—were less novel by origin and intention than by involuntary adaptation to changing conditions. The first and second were outgrowths of the fair and long bore traces of this origin. The third had antecedents in forms of cooperative enterprise common in the middle ages. Of the expansion of credit much will presently be said. Here it may suffice to note that notwithstanding the widening and multiplying use of bills of exchange and the rapid rise of banking in the seventeenth century, a great deal of trade ran on a cash basis. There was an extensive movement of coin and bullion, partly speculative, partly to settle balances in commodity trade between country and country, but also because sellers demanded to see the color of their monies.

For the greater part of the sixteenth century Antwerp " most renowned merchandizing City that ever was in the World," [1] had been both commodity market and financial center of northern Europe. When misfortune overwhelmed this city late in the century, the sceptre passed to Amsterdam, there to remain through the first half of the eighteenth century. In this period of Amsterdam's supremacy we may see some of the transitions and some of the conservative prepossessions at which we have glanced. Her reign, like those of Venice and Antwerp before her, was the reign of a city—the last in which a veritable empire of trade and credit could be held by a city in her own right, unsustained by the forces of a modern unified state. In another respect Amsterdam's heyday was final: the seventeenth was to be the last century in which the trade of Europe was in greater part still intra-European, and therefore susceptible of domination, as it had been dominated in the past, from a position commanding the crossroads of European—not world—travel.

The succession of Amsterdam to Antwerp had not been determined by obvious advantages of site. The city was built on piles to prevent it from sinking into the marshy soil. The port lay far back from the sea, and was difficult of egress when the wind was easterly. Shallow waters made necessary the use of lighters for loading and unloading ships. Few European ports were in better case on this last point however, and difficulty of access and the aqueous site were compensated by defensibility against attacks whether by land or sea. Texel and Vlie were reasonably protected advance-ports for the assembling of Amsterdam's fleets, and communications by river and canal with other towns of the Netherlands, and with adjoining regions of Germany and France, were unrivalled in this age.

And if any one doubt whether Amsterdam be situate as well and better than any other City of Holland for Traffick, and Ships let out to Freight, let him but please to consider in how few hours (when the

---

[1] [Pieter de la Court], *The True Interest and Political Maxims of the Republick of Holland and West Friesland* (London, 1702), p. 50. This is the first English translation of a treatise on economic policy published anonymously in 1662 as *Interest van Holland ofte Gronden van Hollands Welvaren.* In English and French translations the work was attributed to Johan de Witt, whose contribution was limited to part of one chapter in the second edition.

wind is favourable) one may sail from Amsterdam to all the towns of Friesland, Overyssel, Guelderland and North-Holland, & vice-versa, seeing there is no alteration of Course or Tides needful: And in how short a time, and how cheap and easily one may travel from any of the Towns of South-Holland, or other adjacent Inland Citys to Amsterdam, every one knows.[2]

Making the most of her advantages of position, Amsterdam had built up a thriving trade before the middle of the sixteenth century, and was renowned for the number and size of her ships. This early prosperity, founded on the fisheries and the Baltic trade in which Netherlanders had eclipsed their Hanseatic rivals, broadened to include a carrying and entrepôt trade between northern Europe, principally in grain, timber, pitch, tar, metals, hemp, flax, and fish, and western France, principally in wine and salt. Lodovico Guicciardini in 1561 wrote admiringly of the wealth of Amsterdam merchants,[3] but it is possible that some of the capital which built and freighted ships, and bought up in a few days the cargoes of whole fleets laden with Eastland commodities, may have come from Antwerp; and the shipping of Amsterdam and of other ports in the northern provinces sought employment in the great market on the Scheldt which had little shipping of its own. In the middle years of the sixteenth century Amsterdam seems to have had little surplus capital in excess of the needs of her own trade and the ships that carried it. Sir Thomas Gresham, who knew continental money markets well, thought of Amsterdam, if we may judge from his correspondence, only as a place in which to buy wainscoting.[4] The city was known to be well-stocked with grain, lumber, and fish, but had yet to become a general

[2] *Ibid.*, p. 56. On the port of Amsterdam, see C. G. 'T Hooft, "De Wording van Amsterdam als Zeehaven," *Jaarboek van het Genootschap Amstelodamum* (1930), XXVII, 3 ff.

[3] Lodovico Guicciardini, *Discrittione di tutti i paesi bassi . . .* (Anversa, 1567), pp. 184-185. Returns from a capital levy on all monied and propertied men in 1585 testify to the character of Amsterdam's trade and to the still modest scale of the city's wealth. The highest tax (f. 210) was paid by an iron-dealer, while grain-, wood-, and cloth-traders predominate in the upper brackets. For an analysis of the returns and an historical introduction, see J. G. van Dillen, *Amsterdam in 1585 het Kohier der Capitale Impositie van 1585* (Amsterdam, 1941).

[4] John William Burgon, *The Life and Times of Sir Thomas Gresham* (2 vols., London, 1839), II, 117. This is the only mention of Amsterdam in Gresham's correspondence.

mart like Antwerp or Hamburg where merchants might confidently expect to find all kinds of commodities in commercial quantities. When Guicciardini wrote, Amsterdam had no direct sea-borne trade with Mediterranean or with transoceanic lands. Her burgher class was prospering, but there was no group of conspicuously wealthy men in the ascendant. Amsterdam merchants, having no bourse in which to do business, met out of doors in good weather, and in a chapel in bad. The city had as yet no banks, only a licensed *tafel van leening* or ' lombard,' lending money on pawns at usurious rates. Exchange usages were borrowed from Antwerp, but hard cash was probably the rule in business transactions. Amsterdam's industries, compared with those of Flemish cities, were undeveloped.[5]

From this chrysalis of economic simplicity Amsterdam emerged—somewhat abruptly, as it seemed to contemporaries —in the quarter-century covering the last fifteen years of the sixteenth century and the first decade of the seventeenth, to enter upon a metropolitan and cosmopolitan career. Antwerp fell to the Duke of Parma in 1585. Her port was closed, and the noble cities of Flanders and Brabant were isolated and impoverished. Seville and Lisbon were officially barred to rebel Hollanders, and though the latter were willing to run great risks for the sake of great profits in trade to enemy ports, losses were sometimes catastrophic. Trade with France was dislocated by the religious wars. In the face of these changes and dangers Dutch merchants sought direct access to Italy, Turkey, Guinea, the Americas, the Far East, and after the accession of the first Romanoff tsar captured first place in the trade of Russia despite the privileged position of the English Muscovy Company. This rapid commercial expansion was stimulated and in part enabled by an influx of thousands of refugees exiled from the ruined cities of the southern provinces, from Poland and Germany, Spain, Portugal, France, and England.

Several towns of Holland and Zeeland benefitted by this new wealth-making skill and energy, but it was Amsterdam that drew most active recruitment from it.[6] In a country

[5] Van Dillen, *Amsterdam in 1585*, pp. xiii ff.

[6] Admissions to the freedom of the city *(poorterschap)* rose from no more than 344 in the five years, 1575-1579, to 2,768 in the five-year period 1615-

trampled and shattered by war, Amsterdam was reckoned impregnable. The hopeful state of commerce and shipping attracted business men from other lands. In an age when even enlightened communities suppressed religious nonconformity and discriminated against aliens, Amsterdam's gates stood open to all religions and nationalities.[7] The status of *poorter* (citizen) could be acquired at a cost of f. 8 until 1622, when it was raised to f. 14.[8] Though required for admission to gilds, and to certain occupations which included retail trade, its privileges seem not to have been consistently enforced.[9] In admitting foreign craftsmen Amsterdam compromised with gild opposition, found housing for newcomers, and offered inducements to masters deemed capable of starting new industries or improving techniques in those already established.[10]

1619. (*Bronnen tot de Geschiedenis van het Bedrijfsleven en het Gildewezen van Amsterdam,* ed. J. G. van Dillen [Rijks Geschiedkundige Publicatiën, groote serie, nos. 69, 78, 's-Gravenhage, 1929, 1933 (in progress)], I, xxiv; II, xxxii.) Places of origin (to 1606) and occupations represented in the influx have been analyzed in tables by the editor. (*Ibid.,* I, xxxiii ff, xxxvi ff.) Since in all probability most of these new *poorters* were heads of families, and since for many ways of earning a living *poorterschap* was not required, the rise in the figure of admissions affords only a slight indication of the total increase in the city's population through immigration in the half-century following the Union of Utrecht. Dr. Leonie van Nierop's examination of Amsterdam marriage statistics for the years 1586-1601 bears out this indication as to both the sudden spurt of the population as a whole, and the large part in that increase contributed by Antwerp and other towns of Brabant and Flanders. (" De Bruidegoms van Amsterdam," *Tijdschrift voor Geschiedenis* [1934], XLIX, 149 ff.)

[7] The religious liberalism of Amsterdam, though remarkable in this century, was marred by the dark, semi-political episode of the Remonstrant persecution (1617-1619), and by discrimination against Roman Catholics and Jews, though treatment of the latter group was conspicuously tolerant for the time.

[8] Van Dillen, *Bedrijfsleven,* I, xxii-xxiii; II, xxxii.

[9] Foreign trade and most wholesale occupations were open to non-*poorters,* as were also the fairly numerous industries not organized in gilds. Repeated admonitions by the municipal council (*Vroedschap*) calling for observance of burgher right in the reserved occupations suggest that violations were frequent. *Ibid.,* I, 148, 373, 374, 409; see also, *Handvesten; ofte Privilegien ende Octroyen; mitsgaders Willekeuren, Costuimen, Ordonnantien en Handelingen der Stad Amstelredam . . .,* ed. Hermanus Noordkerk (3 vols., Amstelredam, 1748), I, 138-139.

[10] Among the undertakings which received encouragement of one kind or another from the municipal government in the period 1612-1632, were silk-finishing, cloth-making, cloth-dressing with use of the 'hot press,' leather-gilding, glass-blowing, the manufacture of mirrors, salt-refining, shipbuilding, and the setting out of busses to take part in the herring fishery. (Van Dillen, *Bedrijfsleven,* II, xv.) This policy was continued in the second half of the

In course of time regular shipping services connected Amsterdam with the chief trading towns in the United Provinces, with several cities in the southern Netherlands and northwestern Germany, and with Rouen and London. Postal services were extended to meet the needs of trade. Thus port and market were made accessible over a lengthened radius. The *Vroedschap,* governing council of the city, strove to better the condition of the currency and to provide security for capital. Special courts were set up to handle commercial, maritime, and insurance causes.

Foreigners observed Amsterdam's rise to supremacy in world trade with surprise not unmixed with resentment. Suddenly, as it seemed, the city was there.[11] The chamber of assurance was set up in 1598; the United East India Company was chartered in 1602; a new bourse was begun in 1608, and in 1616 the Vroedschap resolved to erect a special bourse for transactions in grain; the exchange bank was founded in 1609, and a lending bank in 1614. Revenue from customs more than doubled between 1589 and 1611.[12] Population soared; reckoned at about 30,000 in 1567, and not greatly in excess of that figure in 1585, it had mounted to 105,000 by 1622, to 115,000 by 1630, and may have passed 200,000 before the end of the third quarter of the century.[13] To accommodate these num-

century, reaching a numerical climax in the reception of some 2,042 French Protestants admitted to *poorterschap* in the decade following 1681. (Leonie van Nierop, "Stukken betreffende de Nijverheid der Refugiés te Amsterdam," *Economisch-historisch Jaarboek; Bijdragen tot de Economische Geschiedenis van Nederland* . . . [1921], VII, 147 ff.; *ibid.* [1923], IX, 157 ff. See also, *Correspondance Administrative sous le règne de Louis XIV* . . ., ed. G. B. Depping [Collection de Documents Inédits sur l'Histoire de France . . ., première série, histoire politique, 4 vols., Paris, 1850-1855], III, 701-702.)

[11] Thus John Wheeler in 1601 mentioned Amsterdam along with other "new upstarte townes in Holland" (*A Treatise of Commerce* . . . ed. G. B. Hotchkiss [The Facsimile Text Society, 5th ser., vol. II, New York, 1931], p. 37); and Antoine de Montchrétien in 1615 contrasted Amsterdam and Middelburg as they were then, " *grosses de peuple, comblées de marchandises, plaines d'or et d'argent,"* with their relative insignificance some twenty-five to thirty years earlier (*Traicté de l'Œconomie Politique* . . ., ed. Th. Funck-Brentano [Paris, 1889], p. 143).

[12] H. Brugmans, *Opkomst en Bloei van Amsterdam* (Amsterdam, 1911), pp. 108 ff.

[13] *Ibid.,* pp. 107-108; Van Dillen, *Bedrijfsleven,* I, xxv-xxvi; and by the same, " Het Bedrijfsleven van Amsterdam in de achttiende eeuw," *Zeven Eeuwen Amsterdam,* ed. A. E. d'Ailly (5 vols., Amsterdam, 1942-1948), IV, 77; Van Nierop, " De Bruidegoms van Amsterdam," *Tijdschrift,* XLIX, 140-141.

bers the town was repeatedly enlarged at great cost in pile-driving and fortification, and in canal- and bridge-building. Visitors came from all parts of Europe to marvel at the wealth, beauty, and populousness of this queenly city. As early as 1600 the duc de Rohan declared that Amsterdam had no equal in Europe for wealth and beauty save Venice only.[14] Adam Olearius, who had travelled in the Far East in the late thirties, heard men speak of Amsterdam " even in the Indies."[15]

The primacy of the city was threefold: as shipping center, as commodity market, and as market for capital, Amsterdam came to surpass all other European towns. It is difficult to say which aspect of her greatness was most substantial, or to dissociate one from dependence on the other two. Shipping was the city's oldest productive asset of more than local consequence. In the mid-fifteenth century Philip the Good of Burgundy had referred to Amsterdam as *" le notable port, la ville la plus marchande de tout notre pays al Hollande."* [16] In the sea war waged against the Hanseatic cities of the Baltic from 1438 to 1441, Amsterdam was said to have furnished more than twenty fighting ships, a number which exceeded those contributed by all the other cities of Holland and Zeeland combined.[17] By the mid-sixteenth century a foreign visitor was already likening to a ' forest ' the close-thronging masts and spars of the shipping in Amsterdam's port [18]—a simile which was to recur in many subsequent descriptions. An Englishman who came to the city in 1586 in the train of the Earl of Leicester, wrote: " There belongeth to this towne a thousand ships, the least of the number of a hundreth tonne, besydes numbers of other shipps and lesser vessalls. . . . They travill furth of most partes to yt, being furnished in a manner for all traydes." [19] Mindful of the easy roundness of

[14] *Voyage du Duc de Rohan, faict en l'an 1600, . . .* (Amsterdam, 1646), pp. 162 ff.

[15] Adam Olearius, *The Voyages and Travels of the Ambassadors sent by Frederick Duke of Holstein to the Great Duke of Muscovy . . . Faithfully rendered into English by John Davies . . .* (2d ed., London, 1669), p. 229.

[16] 'T Hooft, " De Wording van Amsterdam als Zeehaven," *Jaarboek,* XXVII, 5.

[17] *Ibid.,* p. 21.

[18] *Reizigers te Amsterdam beschrijvende lijst van reizen in Nederland door vreemdelingen vóór 1850 . . .* ed. J. N. Jacobsen Jensen (Amsterdam, 1919), p. 4.

[19] *Correspondence of Robert Dudley, Earl of Leycester, during his govern-*

figures uttered in the sixteenth—or the seventeenth—century, we may take this to mean that Amsterdam was frequented by an impressive number of impressively large ships. It was precisely in this period of the city's swift rise to metropolitan stature that Dutch shipyards began turning out a carrier known as the flute (*fluit*), a cargo ship cheaply worked and of good sailing qualities. The success of the flute placed the carriage of a large part of European trade, particularly in bulky and heavy commodities, in Dutch hands, and the freights in Dutch pockets.[20] The type did not originate in Amsterdam, and we have no means of knowing whether she was a great builder of flutes, or merely supplied by a leap of her Norway trade much of the timber and plank for building them. Growth of shipbuilding and ship-freighting in Amsterdam is substantiated by the fact that in 1580-1604, 1,083 persons concerned with the building or the operation of ships were admitted to *poorterschap*. It is significant that a large majority of these—677 out of the 745 whose previous places of residence were recorded—were not exiles from foreign countries but came from towns in the northern Netherlands, most of them from North Holland and Friesland.[21] Evidently such employments were being better rewarded in Amsterdam than in the smaller maritime towns and villages. A sawmill, invention of the late sixteenth century prompted by the demand for plank for houses and ships, was in operation in Amsterdam from the year 1598, and when the original owner's twenty-year monopoly of mechanical sawing ran out in 1619,

---

ment of the Low Countries, in the years 1585 and 1586, ed. John Bruce (Camden Society, Publications, first ser., XXVII [London, 1844]), p. 477.

[20] For the importance of the flute, see Bernhard Hagedorn, *Die Entwicklung der wichtigsten Schiffstypen bis ins 19. Jahrhundert* (Veröffentlichungen des Verein für hamburgische Geschichte, I, [Berlin, 1914]), pp. 102 ff.; G. C. E. Crone, *Onze schepen in de Gouden Eeuw* (2d ed., Amsterdam, 1943), pp. 86 ff. Nicolaes Witsen's work, *Aeloude en Hedendaegsche Scheepsbouw en Bestier* (Amsterdam, 1671), has scale drawings of flutes, plates lx-lxi. On the supremacy of Dutch, and especially of Amsterdam shipping in the Norway timber trade, and in the carriage of Baltic exports, see Johan Schreiner, "Die Niederländer und die Norwegische Holzausfuhr im 17. Jahrhundert," *Tijdschrift voor Geschiedenis* (1934), XLIX, 306 ff., 322; and Aksel E. Christensen, *Dutch trade to the Baltic about 1600 . . .* (The Hague, 1941), *passim.*

[21] Van Dillen, *Bedrijfsleven,* I, xxviii, xxxix, liii-liv; Van Nierop, "De Bruidegoms van Amsterdam," *Tijdschrift,* XLIX, 333.

sawmills multiplied rapidly on the outskirts of the city.[22] But in Zaandam they were more numerous still, and it may be that even in the early years of the seventeenth century Amsterdam shipwrightry was concentrating on turning out large and powerful types, leaving however unwillingly the construction of cargo-ships to the villages along the Zaan and other places where it could be done more cheaply.[23]

Wherever built, the flutes flocked to earn their freights in the service of the metropolitan port. Pieter de la Court was to point out that a great commodity market, capable of buying up the cargoes of whole fleets, and of providing return cargoes as promptly, was an important factor in keeping down freight rates, and in attracting shipping both Dutch and foreign, " So that the English and Flemish merchants &c. do oft-times know no better way to transport their Goods to such Foreign Parts as they design, than to carry them first to Amsterdam, and from thence to other places." [24]

As a commodity market Amsterdam rounded out her position after the fall of Antwerp to that of general emporium. She purveyed everything, from *objets d'art* which attracted foreign visitors to her shops, to fleets ready to fight.[25] The commodities bought and sold on her bourse were staples of world trade; their range and assortment were standards to be consulted in lesser markets; and Amsterdam prices served as indices to commercial Europe. Price lists were printed weekly from 1585, and may have circulated even earlier. In 1613 the sworn brokers of the city were charged with compiling an official list to which anyone could subscribe for f. 4 a year. Recently searched out and studied by Dr. Nicolaes Wilhelmus Posthumus as the basis of his history of Nether-

[22] G. J. Honig, " De molens van Amsterdam," *Jaarboek Amstelodamum* (1930), XXVII, 95 ff.

[23] See below, pp. 69-70.

[24] [La Court], *True Interest*, pp. 35, 38, 115-116; J. C. Westermann, " Beschouwingen over de Opkomst en den Bloei des Handels in de Gouden Eeuw," *Zeven Eeuwen Amsterdam*, ed. D'Ailly, II, 86 ff. The advantage of Amsterdam in this respect was emphasized by Samuel Hayne in *An Abstract of all the Statutes made concerning aliens trading in England* (London, 1685), p. 12. A. E. Christensen has drawn attention to the relative stability of Amsterdam freight rates. (*Dutch Trade*, p. 369.)

[25] On the building and chartering of ships in Amsterdam for the use of foreign powers, see below, pp. 31 ff., 40, 111, 113, 132 ff.

lands prices, they have been found not only in collections in Holland and Zeeland, but in Antwerp, Brussels, Danzig, Copenhagen, Stockholm, Seville, Florence, Vienna, and Batavia.[26]

Merchants who consigned wares to Amsterdam could usually count on quick sale, prompt payment, and broad choice of opportunities to invest the proceeds. If they decided to store their goods in expectation of better prices, they could borrow money on the security of their warehouse receipts. Or they could re-export, paying relatively small duties. Most goods, indeed, came into Amsterdam only to go out again. Expert knowledge of market conditions the world over, skill in appraisal and classification of merchandise, informed brokerage, commission, and wholesale services, credit, insurance, and exchange facilities—all these were to reach their highest development for the seventeenth century in Amsterdam.[27]

Sheer compulsion drew many to this emporium who would have been glad to carry their custom elsewhere. Rulers of England, Spain, France, Denmark, Sweden, Austria, and Russia, who in the course of this century had temporary or permanent agents in Amsterdam to buy or sell for them, were not always happy in their bargains, but accepted them because they could do no better anywhere else. For grain, naval supplies, and munitions, there was no sufficient market but Amsterdam. The whale-oil company founded by Fouquet to combat the Dutch monopoly of the trade in whale products bought train and fins in Amsterdam instead of toilsomely catching whales.[28] Later, Colbert was disconcerted to learn

[26] N. W. Posthumus, *Nederlandsche Prijsgeschiedenis, deel I: Goederenprijsen op de Beurs van Amsterdam, 1585-1914* . . . (Leiden, 1943), introduction. Similar lists were printed in a few other cities in which there was market trading in commodities, e.g., in London from about 1670, but none of these rivalled Amsterdam's list in influence, the prices there being based on a greater volume of transactions and a greater number of commodities. Varieties and prices cited in the *Dictionnaire Universel de Commerce* (see chap. I, n. 35 below) were derived from these lists.

[27] For a general account of the Amsterdam market: T. P. van der Kooy, *Hollands Stapel Markt en haar Verval* (Amsterdam, 1931). On the credit available to Amsterdam merchants on the security of their stocks of commodities: Z. W. Sneller, *Rotterdams Bedrijfsleven in het Verleden* (Amsterdam, 1940), p. 161.

[28] S. Elzinga, *Het Voorspel van den Oorlog van 1672* (Haarlem, 1926), pp. 161-162; *Brieven aan Johan de Witt,* eds. Robert Fruin and N. Japikse (Wer-

that his fledgling Cie. du Nord, designed to capture Amsterdam's Baltic trade, was making up its cargoes in that city.[29] Later still, the French Guinea Company found the pull of the Amsterdam market irresistible even when France was at war with the Dutch republic.[30] The king of Sweden's most valuable asset, his stock of copper, was piled up in Amsterdam warehouses.[31] The Habsburg emperor's most valuable asset, his stock of quicksilver from the Idrian mines, was stored in Amsterdam.[32] The Danish Salt Company sold its salt in Amsterdam against the intention of its charter.[33] The Merchant Adventurers of England, clamoring for punitive action against the city because of its encouragement to interlopers in the cloth trade, concluded their petition: " But the Marchants Adventurers doe humbly pray that they may not be nominated as instruments, to procure the execution of these Courses against those of Amsterdam, in regard that their estate lyes now in Holland, and much thereof in that Towne." [34] Even in the first half of the eighteenth century Amsterdam, though diminished by wars, by mercantilist restrictions at home and abroad which tended to discourage entrepôt trade, and by the competition of ports better placed for oceanic commerce, was still first market of continental Europe. " There is no one who does not know," declared the painstaking compiler of the *Dictionnaire Universel de Commerce* (1723), "that the city of Amsterdam is one of the cities with the greatest trade

ken uitgegeven door het Historisch Genootschap [gevestigd te Utrecht], 3rd ser., nos. 42, 44, 2 vols., Amsterdam, 1919, 1922), I, 285.

[29] *Lettres, instructions et mémoires de Colbert*, ed. Pierre Clément (7 vols. in 9, Paris, 1861-1873), II, 481; P. Boissonnade and P. Charliat, *Colbert et la Compagnie de Commerce du Nord (1661-1689)*, (Paris, 1930), pp. 86 ff.

[30] Georges Scelle, *La Traite Négrière aux Indes de Castille* (2 vols., Paris, 1906), II, 230, note; 253-254; Émile Gabory, " La Marine et le Commerce de Nantes," *Annales de Bretagne* (1902), XVII, 271-272. In 1715 merchants of St. Malo trading under the Guinea Company declared they could not carry on their trade without Indian calicoes from Amsterdam. Paul Kaeppelin, *Les Origines de l'Inde français . . . (1664-1719) . . .* (Paris, 1908), p. 601.

[31] See below, pp. 37, 94, 112, 118.

[32] Heinrich Srbik, *Der staatliche Exporthandel Österreichs von Leopold I bis Maria Theresa . . .* (Wien, 1907), *passim*. See below, p. 109.

[33] Axel Nielsen, *Dänische Wirtschaftsgeschichte* [Handbuch der Wirtschaftsgeschichte hgg. von Dr. Georg Brodnitz, Jena, 1933], p. 281.

[34] Copy of a petition of the Governor, Assistants, and Fellowship of the Merchant Adventurers of England, May, 1635, Public Record Office, London, State Papers, domestic, 16/289, no. 91.

that there is in the world, whether by the amount of money remitted by her merchants and bankers to all foreign countries, or by the almost infinite number of commodities with which her warehouses are filled, and which come in and go out unceasingly in the commerce which she carries on even to the ends of the earth." [35]

The strength of Amsterdam as money market grew out of her supremacy as shipping center and commodity market. Because the city's wealth increased rapidly after the fall of Antwerp, Amsterdam was often charged with merely battening on the spoils of her fallen rival. It is true that the addition of much of Antwerp's banking and exchange business, much of her commodity trade, and some part of her varied and accomplished industry to Amsterdam's already attained staple position for northern products and for shipping services, was a contribution not to be minimized. It is possible that the liberal terms offered by Parma to induce the surrender of towns in the southern provinces may have enabled citizens of those towns who were resolved not to return to their Spanish and Catholic allegiance to send or take with them to other countries capital assets of substantial value.[36] The rapid rise to fortune of many of these exiles, not only in Amsterdam and other towns of the unyielding northern provinces, but also in France, Sweden, and England, lends color to the supposition that they did not come empty-handed to their new homes.[37] In Holland and Zeeland we find these newcomers organizing

[35] *Dictionnaire Universel de Commerce . . . ouvrage posthume du Sieur Jacques Savary des Bruslons . . . continué . . . par M. Philemon Louis Savary . . .* (3 vols. in 4, Paris, 1723). Translated from the article on "Agent de Banque et de Change," I, 46.

[36] For the generous terms offered by Parma, see Van Nierop, *Tijdschrift,* XLIX, 155. Louis de Geer's father, leaving Liège for the northern provinces in 1596, would seem to have managed the transfer of some part of his fortune to his new place of residence, and to have made a not altogether unsatisfactory disposition of the rest. (Froukje Breedvelt-Van Veen, *Louis de Geer 1587-1652* [Amsterdam, 1935], pp. 1 ff.; George Edmundson, "Louis de Geer," *English Historical Review* [1891], VI, 686.) It is significant, too, that Antwerp capital, despite prohibitions, invested in the United East India Company. (Below, p. 57.)

[37] I have in mind the enterprises of Humphrey Bradley, Jan Hoeufft, and other Netherlanders in France (below, pp. 30, 105-106, 120-121); of a large group in London in the early Stuart period, some of whom are mentioned below, pp. 30, 106-107, 123; of the De Besches, De Geers and Trips in Sweden (below, pp. 36 ff., 111-112) of the Marcelises in Denmark and Hamburg (below, pp. 113-114.)

or participating in joint-stock ventures, which opened the Russian, Mediterranean, and East-Indian trades, sought northeast and northwest passages, amassed fortunes in the munitions trade, and initiated speculative trading in company stocks.[38] Of the 320 greatest depositors in the exchange bank of Amsterdam in its early years, 1609-1611, more than half had come from the southern provinces.[39] The tax returns from the levy of the 200th penny in 1631, indicate that about one-third of the richest Amsterdammers were of southern origin.[40] Flemings and Walloons made notable contributions in fields other than finance and foreign trade. They were numerous in the highly remunerative wholesale cloth trade, and in the production of silks, damasks, and other textiles and adornments ministering to luxury in dress; also in glass-making, diamond-cutting, jewelry, goldsmiths' work, leather-dressing, and sugar-baking. The refinement and diversification of the city's industry date from their coming.[41]

[38] Efforts of Balthasar de Moucheron and his associates to open trade with the East by a northeast passage, were doomed to failure, but the attempt gave impetus to trade with Russia via the White Sea. (J. H. de Stoppelaar, *Balthasar de Moucheron* . . . ['s-Gravenhage, 1901].) Two southern Netherlanders, Dirck van Os and Isaac Le Maire, were among the greatest investors in the United East India Company. The former was also a principal investor in the draining of the Beemster (J. Bouman, *Bedijking, Opkomst, en Bloei van de Beemster* [Purmerend, 1857], pp. 31-32), and the latter, among other titles to a dubious notoriety, organized the first company for systematic speculation in the stock of the East India Company. (Below, p. 77.) That the opening of direct seaborne trade with Italy owed much to the initiative of southern Netherlanders who had transferred their allegiance to the Dutch republic, has been suggested by Z. W. Sneller in "De drie Cargasoenen Rogge van Daniel van der Meulen c.s. Anno 1592 . . .," *Jaarboek Amstelodamum*, (1935), XXXII, 91 ff. On the general subject of the contribution made by Netherlanders from the southern provinces to the trade and industry of the young republic, and especially to Amsterdam, see J. G. van Dillen, "Amsterdam in Bredero's Tijd," *De Gids* (June, 1935), XCIX, part ii, p. 311; also, J. L. M. Eggen, *De Invloed door Zuid-Nederland op Noord-Nederland uitgeoefend op het Eind der XVIᵉ en het Begin der XVIIᵉ Eeuw* [Koninklijke Vlaamsche Academie voor Taal- en Letterkunde], Ghent, 1908, Chs. vi-vii, pp. 133 ff.

[39] Van Dillen, "Amsterdam in Bredero's Tijd,," *De Gids*, XCIX, 311.

[40] *Ibid.*

[41] For the contribution of southern Netherlanders to Amsterdam's industry, see especially Van Dillen, *Bedrijfsleven*, I, xvii, xxxvi. Dr. Van Dillen's tables showing the occupations of persons from the southern provinces admitted to *poorterschap* in Amsterdam in the years 1585-1606, bear out the opinion of the late Henri Pirenne, that the exodus from those provinces, while smaller in numbers than had once been believed, was exceptional in quality, the greater part of these exiles belonging to the literate bourgeoisie, to commerce, or to

The wealth of Marranen (Jews of Portuguese or Spanish origin) who sought refuge in Amsterdam in the late sixteenth and the first quarter of the seventeenth century appears to have been exaggerated. There were only about a hundred households of them in the city in 1610, and these supplied few participants either to the founding of the bank, or to the ventures which opened trade to the East. While able to finance their own commerce with Portugal, Spain, Italy, Barbary, and Brazil —all branches of trade requiring some capital—their resources were evidently not great enough to give weight and mobility to Amsterdam capitalism in its formative years. During the truce with Spain, 1609-1621, and again in the forties when the conquest of Brazil by the Dutch West India Company had opened a congenial field for exploitation, the wealth of Amsterdam Marranen made rapid advances. The momentum thus acquired survived even the loss of Brazil to Portugal. In the second half of the century Amsterdam Jewry became a nerve-center of similar Jewish communities in other trading towns of Europe, in the Levant, Barbary, Brazil, and the West Indies. There were Jews in the silk, sugar, tobacco, and diamond industries, also in publishing, but in none of these did they predominate. The trading in company shares, however, was in greater part in the hands of Portuguese and Spanish speculators. But although there were conspicuously rich Jews living in Amsterdam and the Hague, and the average wealth of members of these communities was probably high, returns from the assessment of the 200th penny in 1674 indicate that Sefardiem wealth was still far inferior to Christian wealth in the same brackets.[42]

the higher ranks of skilled craftsmanship. Henri Pirenne, *Histoire de Belgique* (6 vols., Bruxelles, 1917-1926), IV, 338.

[42] J. G. van Dillen, "De Vreemdelingen te Amsterdam in de Eerste Helft der Zeventiende Eeuw, I: De Portugeesche Joden," *Tijdschrift voor Geschiedenis* (1935), L, 4 ff.; and by the same author: "De Economische Positie en Betekenis der Joden in de Republiek en in de Nederlandsche Coloniale Wereld," *Geschiedenis der Joden in Nederland,* ed. Hendrik Brugmans and A. Frank (Amsterdam, 1940), I, 561 ff. For views which would allow much greater importance to the Portuguese and Spanish communities in Amsterdam, even in the early decades of the century, see M. Wolff, "De Eerste Vestiging der Joden te Amsterdam, hun Politieke en Economische Toestand," *Bijdragen voor Vaderlandsche Geschiedenis en Oudheidkunde* (1910), 4th ser., IX, 365 ff.; *ibid.* (1911), X, 134 ff., 354 ff.; Izak Prins, *De Vestiging der Marranen in*

New capital from profits derived from transoceanic trades probably did not reach proportions which would make it concretely effective in the city's business before the early years of the seventeenth century, but the stimulating impact of the new opportunities was promptly felt. The French envoy, Buzanval, noted the excited haste with which Dutch merchants prepared to follow up the return of the first expedition to reach the Far East. "The Portuguese," he observed, "are in danger of not enjoying much longer the riches of the Orient; for all these provinces, which abound in ships and seamen, will run thither as to a fire. . . . It is much that these ships have opened the way to others, and have demonstrated that one has only to venture to become as rich as the Spaniards." [43]

It would be misleading to overstress the new factors in Amsterdam's prosperity and belittle the old. The mainspring of the city's new wealth, as of her earlier modest eminence, seems to have been the trade in grain and naval supplies, and the carriage, storage, and marketing of these and other heavy goods. Circumstances—famine, war, and the altered technique of warfare which called for more and bigger guns, sea adventure which called for more, bigger, and better-armed ships—greatly increased the demand for goods and services which Amsterdam was equipped to supply. Antwerp had never been primarily interested in the trade in bulky commodities, having neither shipping to move it, nor adequate storage facilities. The grain trade was, as De Witt was to say in 1671, "source and root of the most notable commerce and navigation of these lands." [44] Severe dearth in southern Europe in the last decade of the sixteenth century, and intermittently in western Europe in the early decades of the seventeenth, culminating in the famine years of the early thirties, spelled golden profits to

Noord-Nederland in de Zestiende Eeuw (Amsterdam, 1927); Herbert I. Bloom, The Economic Activities of the Jews of Amsterdam in the Seventeenth and Eighteenth Centuries (Williamsport, Pa., 1937); A. M. Vaz Dias, "De Deelname der Marranen in het Oprichtingskapitaal der Oost-Indische Compagnie," Jaarboek Amstelodamum (1936), XXXIII, pp. 43 ff.

[43] Mémoires et Correspondance de Duplessis-Mornay, ed. A. D. de la Fontenelle de Vaudoré and P. R. Anguis (12 vols., Paris, 1824-1825), VII, 327. (Translation.)

[44] F. N. Sickenga, Bijdrage tot de Geschiedenis der Belastingen in Nederland (Leiden, 1864), p. 211.

Amsterdam.[45] Grain provided cargoes and paid freights to keep Amsterdam's merchant marine moving, and so made possible cheap transport of commodities less ship-filling in bulk. Scarcity in any considerable part of Europe was reflected in high grain prices on the Amsterdam bourse, high freights, and consequent stimulation to the city's trade as a whole. Years of plenty had the opposite effect, as Sir William Temple pointed out, when a succession of good harvests over a large part of Europe in the late sixties depressed this key trade.[46] The composition of the governing council of the city in the late sixteenth and the first quarter of the seventeenth century indicates that most of the fortunes represented in that body had been accumulated in occupations long familiar to Amsterdam, originating in the Baltic trade, the fisheries, shipowning, or in Holland's pastoral industry. Most numerous were traders in grain, wood, herring, stockfish, fish-oils, and butter and cheese; next came those who combined wholesale trade with the working up of raw materials for consumption or export, as dealers in oil and ashes, who had become soap-boilers; flax and hemp traders who had set up rope-walks or sail-cutting workshops.[47] As late as 1666 it was estimated that three-fourths of the capital active on the Amsterdam bourse was engaged in the Baltic trade.[48]

[45] On the stimulus provided to Amsterdam's grain trade by famine conditions in southern Europe towards the close of the sixteenth century and in the early seventeenth, see Wijnand Bunk, *Staathuishoudkundige Geschiedenis van den Amsterdamschen Graanhandel* (Amsterdam, 1856), pp. 27 ff., 74 ff. See also, J. H. Kernkamp, *De Handel op den Vijand 1572-1609* (2 vols., Utrecht, 1931, 1934), *passim;* P. J. Blok, "De Handel op Spanje en het Begin der Groote Vaart," *Bijdragen voor Vaderlandsche Geschiedenis en Oudheidkunde* (1913), series 5, I, 102 ff.; J. H. Kernkamp, "Scheepvaart- en Handelsbetrekkingen met Italie tijdens de Opkomst der Republiek," *Mededeelingen van het Nederlandsch Historisch Instituut te Rome* (1936), series 2, VI, 53 ff., Z. W. Sneller, "De drie Cargasoenen Rogge," *Jaarboek,* XXXII, 89 ff.

[46] *Observations upon the United Provinces of the Netherlands* (1673), reprinted under the direction of G. N. Clark (Cambridge [Eng.], 1932), p. 149. "It is obvious," says A. E. Christensen, "that the Dutch merchant marine was directed by the Baltic goods in bulk" (*Dutch Trade to the Baltic,* p. 369).

[47] Willem van Ravesteyn, *Onderzoekingen over de Economische en Sociale Ontwikkeling van Amsterdam gedurende de 16de en het eerste kwart der 17de Eeuw* (Amsterdam, 1906), bijlage v, pp. 272 ff.

[48] Hendr. C. Diferee, *De Geschiedenis van het Nederlandschen Handel tot den Val der Republiek* (Amsterdam, 1908), p. 177. On capital built up in the Baltic trade, see further: H. Brugmans, "Handel en Nijverheid," *Amsterdam in de Zeventiende Eeuw,* by A. Bredius, H. Brugmans, [and others] (3 vols., 's-Gravenhage, 1897-1904), II, 57; C. F. Sirtema van Grovestins, *Histoire*

Of the nine merchants who met in Amsterdam after Hout-man's return from Lisbon in 1594, and subscribed f. 290,000 for the first voyage to the East, five were Hollanders, one had come from Overyssel, one from Holstein, and two from the southern provinces. The other *vóórcompagniën* organized on the heels of this showed the same preponderance of Holland-ers, the Brabant Company excepted.[49] The United East India Company of 1602 was a merger of the *vóórcompagniën,* and its capital of f. 6,500,000, of which Amsterdam raised f. 3,675,-000, represented the same background of resources.[50] Presum-ably as Dutch in the origin of its capital was the merger of several whaling enterprises in the Noordsche Compagnie char-tered in 1614. Of this capital, half was supplied by a single Amsterdam firm, that of Lambert van Tweenhuysen, which included Netherlanders from both northern and southern prov-inces.[51] Most of the capital invested in the drainage project of the Beemster in 1608-1612, amounting at last to f. 1,492,500, was of genuine Dutch provenance, supplied in large part by officials and magistrates of Amsterdam with a sprinkling of merchants and some participation by officialdom in other towns of Holland.[52]

A factor in the building up of Amsterdam's capital resources, whose precise importance we have no means of estimating, was the saving and investing habit of Hollanders of moderate or

des luttes et rivalités politiques entre les puissances maritimes et la France, durant la seconde moitié du XVIIe siècle (8 vols., Paris, 1851-1854), I, 134.

[49] André-E. Sayous, "Die grossen Händler und Kapitalisten in Amsterdam gegen Ende des sechzehnten und während des siebzehnten Jahrhunderts," *Welt-wirtschaftliches Archiv* (1937), XLVI, 698 ff.

[50] *Ibid.,* pp. 700 ff.

[51] G. W. Kernkamp, "Stukken over de Noordsche Compagnie," *Bijdragen en Mededeelingen* (1898), XIX, 266; S. Muller, *Geschiedenis der Noordsche Compagnie* (Utrecht, 1874), pp. 78 ff.; André-E. Sayous, "Le Rôle d'Amsterdam dans l'histoire du capitalisme commercial et financier," *Revue Historique* (1938), CLXXXIII, 267 ff.

[52] J. Bouman, *Bedijking, Opkomst en Bloei van de Beemster,* pp. 263 ff. For the names and qualities of the entrepreneurs and proprietors, *ibid.,* pp. 33 ff., 63-64, 78. A brief account of the Beemster with a plan of the area and the names and occupations (or offices) of the principal undertakers was included in *L'Atlas de Gerard Mercator et d'Hondius* (éd. nouvelle, 2 vols., Amsterdam, 1633), I, 380. The strong Amsterdam contingent (19 out of 65) among investors in the draining of the Zijpe in 1597, were also of Holland stock. J. Belonje, "Amsterdam Grondbezit in de Zijpe omstreeks 1600," *Jaar-boek Amstelodamum* (1936), XXXIII, 37-38.

even small means, who in other countries might have aspired to buy or lease farms or other small properties. In Holland there was little land to be had, and that at high price or rent and severely taxed. Therefore savings went into shares in ships or mills, into fishing or trading voyages, into polder enterprises; sometimes into municipal or provincial loans.[53] The disappointment which attended the first attempt to drain the Beemster froze out of a number of such small investors who could put up no more capital for the completion of the undertaking.[54] The large sums subscribed by the chief *participanten* to the United East India Company commonly included a number of small contributions placed in their hands by various *medestaanders* (supporters), presumably relatives and friends.[55] Sir William Temple, speaking of Hollanders in general, observed: " Their common Riches lye in every Man's having more than he spends; or, to say it properly, In every Man's spending less than he has coming in, be that what it will." [56] As in nineteenth-century France, so in seventeenth-century Holland this substratum of small savings on which the entrepreneur could draw, played at least a modest role in capitalist undertakings.

There can be little doubt that Amsterdam capitalism received stimulus from the war-spending of European princes and governments, perhaps in the sixteenth century, certainly and increasingly in the seventeenth—a century of wars. While Amsterdam may not have been directly concerned in the complicated subsidy arrangements contracted with the States General by Elizabeth of England and Henri IV of France, she was indirectly concerned as the town near the seat of war best able to furnish food and arms to French and English auxiliaries and to handle exchange. The Earl of Leicester was taking up money there in 1587, and in the following year Henry Killigrew, English member of the republic's council of state, mentioned receiving money from England by bills of exchange on Amsterdam.[57] Funds remitted by the first Stuart kings for the

---

[53] See below, p. 80.

[54] Sayous, "Die grossen Händler und Kapitalisten," *Weltwirtschaftliches Archiv*, XLVI, 704-705.

[55] *Ibid.*, p. 699.

[56] *Observations upon the United Provinces of the Netherlands*, p. 102.

[57] *Calendar of State Papers, foreign series . . . 1587*, ed. S. C. Lomas and

recovery of the Palatinate and for assistance to the king of Denmark were sent via Amsterdam.[58] So too were subsidies and bribes by which the governments of Louis XIII and Louis XIV financed their allies.[59]

Provisioning of troops was a natural outgrowth of the Amsterdam grain market and of successive wars fought on, near, or within the frontiers of the Netherlands. While the United Provinces were struggling for their independence, Holland supplied not only their own forces in the field, but now and then those of Leicester, and intermittently at least those of Spain in the southern provinces.[60] During the English civil wars grain

A. B. Hinds (London, 1929), p. 427; *ibid., July-Dec., 1588,* ed. R. B. Wernham (London, 1936), p. 253.

[58] These transactions were handled by Philip Burlamachi as paymaster for the forces in England, and by his kinsman, Julian Burlamachi, deputy paymaster in the Netherlands for troops sent over to Mansfeld and for the assistance of Denmark. Funds for the pay and maintenance of these troops, and later for shuttling back the remnant of them to be used in Buckingham's Cadiz expedition, were remitted by bills of exchange drawn for the most part on Amsterdam, with which city Burlamachi maintained close business relations through his brother-in-law, Philip Calandrini. (See below, pp 106-107, 123 n.) Part of the expenses of the original expedition had been unwillingly advanced by the States General and in the darkening state of Stuart finances, was never repaid.

[59] Richelieu had two agents with Amsterdam connections. The more important was Jan or Jean Hoeufft, member of a Brabançon family settled in France. Naturalized in 1601 he rose to become counsellor-secretary to Louis XIII, an office which covered useful banking services to the Crown. At the same time he acted as commissioner of the States of Holland at the French court. In his exchange business on Amsterdam he drew on Mattheus (Mathieu) Hoeufft, presumably a brother. Glimpses of Hoeufft as paymaster of French and Swedish armies and purchasing agent, also of the somewhat shadier aspects of Richelieu's remissions to Amsterdam through Hoeufft's hands, may be gathered from the cardinal's correspondence. (*Lettres, instructions diplomatiques et papiers d'état du Cardinal de Richelieu,* ed. M. Avenel [Collection de Documents Inédits sur l'Histoire de France, 1re série, Histoire Politique, 8 vols., Paris, 1835-1877], V-VIII, *passim.*) For further mention of Hoeufft, see below, pp. 105-106, 121. Richelieu also employed Alfonse Lopez, an exile from Spain, in transactions in Amsterdam, mainly as purchasing agent. (See below, 38 n., 106 n.) Both Hoeufft and Lopez were used by Mazarin at the beginning of his ministry in the same employments in which they had served Richelieu. For an allusion to the payment of Louis XIV's subsidies to German and northern rulers by letters of exchange on Amsterdam, see P. Boissonnade and P. Charliat, *Colbert et la Compagnie de Commerce du Nord (1661-1689),* p. 121.

[60] *Calendar of State Papers, foreign series, 1585-1586,* ed. S. C. Lomas (London, 1921), pp. 184-185; *ibid., domestic series, 1591-1594,* ed. M. A. E. Green (London, 1867), pp. 115, 574; *Correspondence of Robert Dudley, Earl of Leycester,* p. 426; J. H. Kernkamp, *De Handel op den Vijand, passim;* Sayous,

George Downing written in 1661 one may infer that insurance of the Spanish treasure fleet was placed in that city, though these policies may have been taken out by Amsterdam merchants interested in the treasure carried.[88] We hear, too, of Copenhagen ships being insured in Amsterdam.[89] The European reputation enjoyed by the city as a place in which marine insurance was handled in an honest and businesslike way, continued well into the eighteenth century.[90]

In still another direction war opened opportunities to Amsterdam capitalists. Until late in the sixteenth century the city had small importance as a market for arms and munitions, being excelled in that capacity by both Antwerp and Hamburg. The war against Spain, and later the Thirty Years' War, created an insatiable demand for munitions to meet not only Dutch military and naval needs and those of their allies, but also (in accord with Dutch practice) those of the enemy.[91] Amsterdam's succession to Antwerp was promoted by easy communications with Liége and Namur via the Maas, deep in enemy country though they lay, and with near-by German metallurgical centers, Aachen, Solingen, and Cornelimunster. In 1619 a company of Amsterdam merchants invested in a foundry for casting guns in Thuringia.[92] Guns of heavy calibre—in the esti-

mercie te Amsterdam, 1663-1665," *Bijdragen en Mededeelingen* (1897), XVIII, 194, 301 ff.

[88] T. H. Lister, *Life and Administration of Edward, first Earl of Clarendon* . . . (3 vols., London, 1837-1838), III, 144.

[89] Nielsen, p. 199.

[90] Jean-Pierre Ricard, *Le Négoce d'Amsterdam* . . . (Rouen, 1723), pp. 248-249; Jacques Le Moine de l'Espine, *De Koophandel van Amsterdam,* enlarged and improved by Isaac Le Long (7th ed., Rotterdam, 1753), pp. 39-40. Both of these works are revisions of the original *Le Négoce d'Amsterdam ou Traité de sa Banque* by Le Moine de l'Espine, first published in Amsterdam in 1694.

[91] Much information on the trade in arms and munitions with the southern provinces and with Spain is scattered through the two volumes of Kernkamp's *De Handel op den Vijand.* When the twelve years' truce with Spain came to an end in 1621, the munitions trade with the enemy was resumed with energy. M. G. de Boer, "Een Amsterdamsche 'Lorrendraaier' Celio Marselis," *Jaarboek Amstelodamum* (1941), XXXVIII, 37 ff.; E. Baasch, "Der Verkehr mit Kriegsmaterialen aus und nach den Hansestädten . . .," *Jahrbücher für Nationalökonomie und Statistik* (1932), CXXXVII, pp. 541 ff.

[92] Van Dillen, *Bedrijfsleven,* II, 324, 326. In 1624 Louis de Geer stated that he had placed orders for supplying arms to the Swedish army "au pays de Liège, Coulogne, Namur, Aix, Sollingen et autres lieux où les ouvriers se tiennent . . ." (E. W. Dahlgren, *Louis de Geers Brev och Affärshandlingar 1614-1652* [Stockholm, 1934], p. 77.) We hear of a Dutchman, Paulus van

mation of that age—were imported from England during the reign of Elizabeth and, with more difficulty in obtaining licenses, under the early Stuarts.[93] The Baltic trade brought in potash for making gunpowder, the Italian trade sulphur, and saltpetre could be had from several European countries and from the East Indies.

The striking phase of Amsterdam's international trade in arms opened shortly after the truce of 1609, when three merchants, Elias Trip, Steven Gerard, and Louis de Geer, brothers-in-law and all of Liégeois families domiciled in Holland, began to specialize in the munitions trade and made Amsterdam their business headquarters about the year 1615. It was in this year that De Geer made his first visit to Sweden to procure ordnance for the States General. There he met Willem de Besche, another Liégeois exile, who had already leased mining properties in Formark and was beginning to smelt iron. In 1619, with the cooperation of De Besche, De Geer undertook the development of iron and copper mines in Finspong, the first of a succession of leases and purchases which were to make him one of the wealthiest men in Europe. While continuing to furnish his customers with arms from the older manufacturing centers of Liége, the Rhenish towns, and England, De Geer in partnership

Houten operating a gun foundry near San Sebastian in Spain, where in 1656 he was filling an order for cannon placed by the Admiralty of Amsterdam. (*A Collection of the State Papers of John Thurloe, Esq.* . . ., ed. T. Birch [7 vols., London, 1742], IV, 642.) For a similar Dutch attempt to set up a gun-foundry in Wales, see below, p. 121.

[93] There are frequent allusions in the *Calendar of State Papers, domestic series,* to the transport of ordnance to the Netherlands, from the year 1584 to the end of Elizabeth's reign. In 1603 the Venetian ambassador gave an exaggerated account of this dependence on England: Up to now, he wrote, owing to the small distance of only one hundred miles of sea, they have been able to supply themselves from England with all necessaries, more especially with artillery—which they cannot make over there, nor can they recast a single piece—cannon-balls, powder, saltpetre, and above all men and arms. (*Calendar of State Papers, and Manuscripts relating to English Affairs* . . . *in the Archives and Collections of Venice* . . . *1603-1607,* ed. H. F. Brown [London, 1900], p. 50.) A bill to prohibit export of ordnance was introduced in the House of Commons in 1614 on the ground that "the Hollanders are nowe so stronge by reason of our English Ordinance that they beginne to outbrave the Englishe. . . ." (*Commons Debates 1621,* eds. Wallace Notestein, Frances Helen Relf, and Hartley Simpson [7 vols., New Haven, 1935], VII, 637.) But both Elias Trip and Louis de Geer were able to obtain licences to export. In 1627 De Geer expressed hope that his Swedish foundries could cast enough guns to enable him to dispense with English ordnance. (Dahlgren, p. 118.)

with De Besche established smelters and foundries on his Swedish properties, recruited skilled metal-workers and gunfounders, and in the second quarter of the century raised Sweden to first rank in the production of munitions. His brother Matthias de Geer, and later his nephews, Jacob, Louis, and Hendrick Trip, became owners or lessees of extensive mining properties in Sweden, and several other Amsterdammers invested in similar enterprises in this period. Some of these competed with De Geer in producing pig- and bar-iron, and in the manufacture of some types of arms, but in 1627 De Geer had secured from the crown an exclusive patent for casting iron guns, and this he continued to hold, except for an interval of four years, until 1648 when the Thirty Years' War came to an end. Gerard was in the munitions business for himself, and also acted as De Geer's partner in negotiating contracts, and in managing the Amsterdam end of the business. Elias Trip too conducted an extensive arms trade from Amsterdam. Through his practical monopoly of exports of Swedish copper he was able to keep the coppermasters in Aachen, Namur, and Liége, in his employ. His relations with De Geer, originally friendly and cooperative, became embittered, and in the late years of his life—Trip died in 1636—the two arms kings found difficulty in striking a balance between their common business interests and their mutual dislike.[94]

During the Thirty Years' War De Geer's warehouses in

[94] There are biographies of Louis de Geer by Froukje Breedvelt-van Veen, *Louis de Geer 1587-1652* (Amsterdam, 1935) by E. W. Dahlgren, *Louis de Geer hans Lif och Verk* (2 vols., Uppsala, 1923), and by Charles Frederic Wiberg, *Louis de Geer et la colonisation Wallonne en Suède* (Liège, 1876); also a brief sketch by George Edmundson in the *English Historical Review* (1891), VI, 685 ff. De Geer's letters, edited by Dahlgren, have been referred to in the two preceding notes. Of considerable importance for a study of the arms trade centering in Amsterdam are: " Amsterdamsche Notarieele Acten betreffende den Koperhandel," ed. J. G. van Dillen, *Bijdragen en Mededeelingen* (1937), LVIII, 211 ff.; and J. E. Elias, "Contract tot Oprichting van een Zweedsch Factorie-comptoir te Amsterdam in 1663," *ibid.* (1903), XXIV, 356 ff. A brief account of Jacob, Louis, and Hendrick Trip, nephews of both Elias Trip and Louis de Geer, who in 1634 founded a firm to carry on the munitions trade, and later engaged in the munitions industry in Sweden, will be found in Johan E. Elias, *De Vroedschap van Amsterdam, 1578-1795* (2 vols., Haarlem, 1903, 1905), II, 547-548. For Steven Gerard, who was trading in arms as early as 1614, we must depend on the biographies of De Geer. On Amsterdam's capture of the trade in arms and munitions from Hamburg, see E. Baasch, *Jahrbücher*, CXXXVII, pp. 541 ff.

Amsterdam supplied not only the armies of Gustavus Adolphus and the States General, but also those of Denmark, France, and the auxiliary troops commanded by Ernst Count Mansfeld, Christian of Brunswick, and John of Saxe-Weimar.[95] Richelieu's purchases between 1627 and 1641 included copper, saltpetre, gunpowder, shot, muskets and cannon.[96] Venice was a customer of De Geer, and Portugal became one when its population rose against Spain in 1640.[97] England, from which both De Geer and Trip had imported ordnance, was at length obliged to turn to the Amsterdam market. Charles I was buying arms there in the four years preceding the outbreak of the civil war. Some of the shipments were made by De Geer, and some by other Amsterdam merchants.[98] At about the same time suspicion was voiced in England that Scottish Covenanters were receiving arms from the same quarter.[99] During the English civil wars Holland, presumably Amsterdam, provided munitions to the royal forces by way of Dunkirk,[100] and later to

[95] Breedvelt-Van Veen, pp. 11 ff.

[96] Richelieu's purchases were negotiated by Lopez, occasionally by Hoeufft (see above, note 60). A memorandum among the cardinal's papers, undated but perhaps of 1638, indicates that Lopez had expended about f. 185,997 *monnaye de Hollande* on such commissions. (*Lettres . . . du Cardinal de Richelieu*, VI, 261.) For correspondence bearing on French munitions orders: *ibid.*, III, 4 ff., 9, 11-12, 56-57; IV, 184; V, 409, 641-642, 985, 997, 1007; VI, 822; VII, 962; Dahlgren, *Louis de Geers Brev*, p. 119. The "Sieur Trip" mentioned once by the cardinal in connection with an order for guns, was probably Pieter Trip, kinsman of Elias Trip, and partner and commission agent of De Geer. (*Lettres . . . du Cardinal de Richelieu*, VII, 962.)

[97] Breedvelt-Van Veen, pp. 12, 87.

[98] Gerard was sending consignments of arms to England in 1617, and again in 1620. In 1621 Louis de Geer furnished estimates—too high, it appeared—for the arming of English troops sent over to assist in the recovery of the Palatinate. (*Calendar of State Papers, domestic series, 1619-1623*, ed. M. A. E. Green [London, 1858], pp. 239-240; *Acts of the Privy Council of England in the Reign of James I, 1619-1621*, ed. J. V. Lyle [London, 1930], pp. 370-371, 384). Some purchases of arms in Holland would seem to have been made a few years later. (J. W. Fortescue, *A History of the British Army* [10 vols., London, 1910-1920], I, 192.) From 1638 there were frequent shipments from Amsterdam. (*Calendar of State Papers, domestic series, 1638-1639,* and *1639,* ed. by John Bruce and W. D. Hamilton [London, 1871, 1873], *passim;* Breedvelt-van, p. 83; De Boer, *Jaarboek,* XXXVIII, 48).

[99] *Calendar of State Papers, domestic series,* 1639, p. 98, Edward Hyde, Earl of Clarendon, *The History of the Rebellion and Civil Wars in England . . .* (7 vols., Oxford, 1849), I, 179.

[100] *Calendar of State Papers, domestic series, 1644-1645,* ed. W. D. Hamilton (London, 1890), pp. 366-367, 387, 466, 480.

Montrose.[101] In 1650 a ship from Holland brought munitions to the Scottish army.[102] From the second quarter of the century Amsterdam was supplying weapons to the Russian tsars, and this commerce continued throughout the seventeenth and into the eighteenth century.[103]

De Geer and Trip were the most successful munitions merchants of their day. In 1628 De Geer and his partners were reputed to have cleared a profit of f. 60,000 on sales of lead, iron, and iron guns; and between 1624 and 1648 he claimed to have made deliveries of war *matériel* to the Swedish armies to the value of rd. 736,080.[104] But the De Geer and Trip interests were not able to monopolize the Amsterdam trade in munitions. . During the war with Spain the States General had insisted that arms and ammunition should not be exported without license, but the colleges of admiralty, and especially that of Amsterdam, were willing to grant licenses with little investigation of the destination to which shipments were bound, or whether they had been properly declared. During the years 1634 and after, the trade seems to have been wide open. From June, 1636, to June, 1637, some thirty licenses were granted which permitted export of 400,000 lbs. of match, 350,000 lbs. of gunpowder, and 180,000 lbs. of sulphur, besides guns, pikes, and muskets in considerable quantity. How much of similar merchandise was smuggled out under cover of these licenses we have no way of knowing.[105] Failure of an attempt by a public-spirited official in 1641 to secure conviction of Celio

---

[101] *Ibid., 1645-1647* (London, 1891), pp. 23, 66; *Calendar of the Clarendon State Papers preserved in the Bodleian Library,* eds. O. Ogle, W. H. Bliss [and others], (4 vols., Oxford, 1869-1932), II, 15-16.

[102] *The Writings and Speeches of Oliver Cromwell . . .,* ed. Wilbur Cortez Abbott, with the assistance of Catherine D. Crane (4 vols., Cambridge [Mass.], 1937-1947), II, 362.

[103] Jacobus Scheltema, *Rusland en de Nederlanden* (4 vols., Amsterdam, 1817), I, 124-125, 177-178; II, 45; III, 158-159; C. C. Uhlenbeck, *Verslag aangaande een Onderzoek in de Archieven van Rusland ten bate der Nederlandsche Geschiedenis* ('s-Gravenhage, 1891), pp. 23 ff.; D. S. van Zuiden, *Bijdrage tot de Kennis van de Hollandsch-Russische Relaties in de 16de-18de Eeuw . . .* (Amsterdam, 1911), pp. 11 ff.

[104] Breedvelt-Van Veen, pp. 84, 93. Dahlgren has estimated that profits reaped by De Geer and his partners from the trade in arms and munitions may have averaged about 40 per cent a year, presumably in the period 1628-1648. (*Louis de Geer, hans Lif och Verk,* I, 309 ff.)

[105] De Boer, *Jaarboek,* XXXVIII, 46 ff.

Marcelis, well-known as a trader in contraband, and suspected of supplying the enemy with munitions via Dunkirk or Hamburg, assured merchants of impunity, even with a good deal of evidence against them.[106]

Although the demand for munitions fell off after the Peace of Westphalia, it became brisk again in the wars of the second half of the century when Russia, the Empire, Brandenburg, Spain, France, Venice, the Sultan, and the Barbary pirates patronized the Amsterdam market. We have the testimony of a Frenchman commissioned to make the purchases, that during the first Franco-Dutch war which opened in 1672, the Dutch provided Louis XIV's armies with all their powder, match, and lead.[107] When the imperial ambassador at the Hague urged the States General to prohibit deliveries of copper, steel, and iron to the Turks and the Barbary states, the reply was, that it was impossible to hinder this traffic, and the emperor would do well to permit exports of metal to Turkey from his own lands.[108] In 1664 a consortium of Amsterdam capitalists was negotiating with the Austrian Hofkammer a project for setting up a *General-proveditorat* which would assume entire responsibility for arming, equipping, and provisioning the imperial army. This failed because the impoverished court could not find sufficient security to satisfy the entrepreneurs.[109] In a more piecemeal way Amsterdam sold saltpetre and gunpowder, siege machines, and even warships to the imperial government.[110] England could normally supply her own munitions needs, but in emergencies had recourse to Amsterdam.[111] The city of Hamburg bought guns for her convoy there in 1686.[112]

Sweden was still the principal source of supply for cannon and ball. In the second half of the century the established De Geer and Trip interests were challenged by later comers, entre-

---

[106] *Ibid.*, p. 45.

[107] *Correspondance des Contrôleurs Généraux des Finances,* ed. De Boislisle, I, 395, note.

[108] Srbik, p. 69.

[109] *Ibid.*, pp. 44, 72, note.

[110] *Ibid.*, pp. 73-74.

[111] G. H. Kurtz, *Willem III en Amsterdam 1683-1685,* (Utrecht, 1928), p. 192; *Calendar of Treasury Papers, 1557-1696,* ed. Joseph Redington (London, 1868), p. 426.

[112] E. Baasch, *Hamburgs Convoyschiffahrt und Convoywesen . . . im 17. und 18. Jahrhundert* (Hamburg, 1896), p. 151.

preneurs and ironmasters, also from Holland, who developed mining properties and engaged in the manufacture of guns. In 1664 four Amsterdammers succeeded in obtaining from the Swedish regency an exclusive patent for exporting cast-iron guns to the Amsterdam market, and formed a *factorie-comptoir* in that city to exploit it.[113] This enterprise on the part of their subjects so alarmed the States of Holland, the second war with England being just around the corner, that they voted to establish a gun-foundry of their own to supply the military and naval requirements of the state. This counter-move was carried out with success, and the Swedish monopoly thereby breached.[114]

Towards the close of the century William Carr, English consul at Amsterdam, observed of the city: " It hath inconceivable Store of all manner of Provisions for War, insomuch, that England and divers other Nations send to Amsterdam to buy Arms, Buff-Coats, Belts, Match, &c. Yea, here are several Shopkeepers who can deliver Arms for four or five Thousand Men, and at a Cheaper rate than can be got any where else. . . ." [115] " This city is very famous for good powder," wrote an English merchant at about the same time, " and no place in the world can afford such a quantity in so short a time." [116] Almost half a century later Amsterdam was still the munitions market of Europe:

The Dutch are the most expert Founders in the World, and furnish most Countries with Ordnance. The German, Spanish, Italian, African,

---

[113] Elias, *Bijdragen*, XXIV, 356 ff.

[114] *Ibid.*, pp. 386-387. The *factorie-comptoir* was still doing business in Amsterdam in 1667, but there were complaints of the poor quality of its merchandise, and it was feeling the competition of new foundries in the Rhenish metallurgical region. Gemeente Oud-Archief, Not. Arch. 3191, Notaris Hendrik Outgers, June 27, 1667.

[115] *A Description of Holland, with some necessary Directions for such as intend to travel through the Province of Holland . . . By an English Gentleman* (London, 1701), p. 17. This work was printed and reprinted in varying versions under varying titles from 1688 through the first quarter of the eighteenth century. The earliest edition I have seen is that of 1693, entitled: *Travels through Flanders, Holland, Germany, Sweden and Denmark written by an English Gentleman who resided many years in Holland in a publick capacity.* There seems no reason to doubt that Carr was the author. In the edition of 1701 the material on Holland was expanded, and that on other countries omitted.

[116] *Calendar of State Papers, domestic series, 1700-1702*, ed. Edward Bateson (London, 1937), p. 524.

and Turkish Troops have their Arms principally from Amsterdam; as also their Cannon, Mortars, Powder, and Lead. What is more, during the last two general Wars, Louis XIV, who thought to carry every Art and Manufacture to its highest Perfection, and particularly all that appertained to the Art Military, was however obliged to the Gunsmiths and Founders of Amsterdam, the Metropolis of an Enemy, for Arms and Ammunition for his Troops.[117]

---

[117] *A Description of Holland: or the Present State of the United Provinces* (London, 1743), p. 236.

CHAPTER II

THE EXCHANGE BANK OF AMSTERDAM—TRADE IN
PRECIOUS METALS—BILLS OF EXCHANGE

The most famous instrument of Amsterdam capitalism in this century was the exchange bank. Founded in 1609, administered under the supervision of the city, it was the first and long the greatest public bank in northern Europe. Confidence in its stability and integrity was a strong attraction to capital both Dutch and foreign.[1] Until the last ten or fifteen years of the sixteenth century Amsterdam's trade had moved in greater part on payments in coin. Printed forms of bills of exchange came into use about the year 1597, and cashier services were then common, but as late as 1608 the city fathers, bent on keeping business on a basis of *klinkende munt,* prohibited both cashier practices and assignments of bills of exchange or other forms of paper credit.[2] By setting up the exchange bank they hoped to restrict the circulation of paper and put down *kassierderij.* They hoped also to remedy the unsatisfactory state of the currency which was attributed to dark arts practiced by exchangers and cashiers. The ordinance which established the bank required that all bills of exchange to the value of f. 600 or more must be paid into the bank; the resulting credits might then be assigned on order. Though the monopoly of exchange and cash-keeping originally vested in the bank was soon relaxed, the greater part of the city's business of a scale and nature to need such services was re-

---

[1] The indispensable work on the bank is the collection of sources, *Bronnen tot de Geschiedenis der Wisselbanken (Amsterdam, Middelburg, Delft, Rotterdam),* ed. J. G. van Dillen [Rijks Geschiedkundige Publicatiën, groote serie, nos. 59, 60], 2 vols., 's-Gravenhage, 1925. Dr. van Dillen has also written several brief accounts of the bank, among them, "The Bank of Amsterdam" in *History of the Principal Public Banks,* edited by him as secretary of the International Committee for the Study of the History of Banking and Credit (The Hague, 1934), pp. 79 ff. An old but informative work on the bank is that of W. C. Mees, *Proeve eener Geschiedenis van het Bankwesen in Nederland gedurende den Tijd der Republik* (Rotterdam, 1838). Seventeenth- and eighteenth-century descriptions of the bank are numerous.

[2] Mees, pp. 21 ff.

corded on the ledgers of the bank. Until 1683 its activities were confined to exchange and deposit banking, which spared it the hazards involved in discounting notes and lending money to individuals. The bank did, however, extend credits to the lending bank from the latter's foundation in 1614 to about the year 1640; and it made advances to the East India Company from the year 1619, and to the city of Amsterdam. But the lending bank had built up capital adequate to its needs before the middle of the century; credits to the East India Company were short-term loans in anticipation of income; and those to Amsterdam did not, until late in the century, exceed the bank's profits to which the city was entitled.[3] At no time was the solvency of the bank endangered by these loans. When the first 'run' occurred in 1672, the institution was saved by its high metallic coverage. The balance sheet of January 31 of that year showed that for the f. 7,201,433 owing its depositors, the bank could produce coin and bullion to the value of f. 6,654,277, and unimpeachable securities for the missing half-million florins.[4]

The bank's standards in handling exchange helped to establish Amsterdam as hub of European exchanges. To the volume and importance of that business we shall presently return. Much of it was transacted out of bank by cash payments, especially in the commercial relations of Dutch towns with one another, with the Hanseatic cities, and with those of East Friesland, Westphalia, Denmark and Sweden. Bills drawn in consequence of more distant trading activities were usually, though not invariably, paid in bank.[5] The availability of the bank for exchange transactions unquestionably exerted a wholesome restraint on private exchangers.

As cashier the bank provided a security and convenience rare in the annals of seventeenth-century banking. No man, observed an English admirer of the bank, would trouble to receive his own money while he had a cashier who cost him nothing, and the security of the city against all robberies and accidents whatsoever; security too against loss by short tale, false, or

[3] Van Dillen, *Bronnen tot de Geschiedenis der Wisselbanken*, I, xi, II, 971 ff.; and by the same authority: "Een Nieuw Licht op de Amsterdamsche Wisselbank?" *Tijdschrift voor Geschiedenis* (1934), XLIX, pp. 31 ff.
[4] Van Dillen, "The Bank of Amsterdam," *History*, pp. 91-92.
[5] Z. W. Sneller, *Rotterdams Bedrijfsleven* (Amsterdam," 1940), pp. 152-153.

clipped money.[6] The number of depositors rose from 708 in 1611, to 2,698 in 1701, and was to continue to increase in the eighteenth century.[7] Deposits rose in the same period from f. 925,562 to 16,284,849 in 1700.[8] The ease with which payments could be made by assigning bank credit, now so commonplace, seemed in the seventeenth century a bewildering form of prestidigitation: the money remained safe in the vaults of the bank even while being paid out again and again in transactions which might span Europe. "Up to this point," wrote a merchant after describing the method of establishing credit, "one sees that there is as much reality in this as there could well be, nothing being more real than ingots of gold, bars of silver, piastres, ducats, ducatons, and suchlike, but the method of payment in bank, as it is called, has not the same reality. One could, on the contrary, call it a veritable illusion; since for the gold and silver taken to the bank it gives only a line of writing in a book. This line may be transferred to another, and this second transfers it to a third . . . and this can go on, so to speak, to infinity." [9]

To acquire prestige as a merchant or man of affairs in Amsterdam it was almost indispensable to have an account in the bank.[10] The list of depositors is in the nature of a roll-call of Amsterdam capitalists. One is struck by the number of names with connotations in international finance: the De Geers and Trips for Sweden; the Marcelises and Joachim Irgens for Denmark-Norway; the Sautijns and Van der Straten for Italy;

[6] Bodleian Library, Oxford, Clarendon MS. 83, f. 419, "Proposall for a Banck of Exchange and Lendinge."

[7] Van Dillen, *Bronnen tot de Geschiedenis der Wisselbanken*, II, 985, table vi.

[8] *Ibid.*, II, 962 ff.

[9] "Mémoire touchant le négoce et la navigation des Hollandois/Dressée à Amsterdam en 1699 au Mois de Juin," communicated by P. J. Blok, who ascribes it tentatively to a Zeeland merchant, Izaak Loysen, *Bijdragen en Mededeelingen* (1903), XXIV, 315-316. (Translation.) How little such assignments of bank credit were known in England as late as 1630 or thereabout, may be inferred from Thomas Mun's description of them as peculiar to the Italians. (*England's Treasure by Forraign Trade,* reprinted from the first edition of 1664 for the Economic History Society, Oxford, 1928, p. 17.)

[10] On this indispensability see the "Mémoire" cited in the preceding note, p. 318, and another assertion of similar tenor in a "Mémoire des Députés du Commerce sur la Proposition de l'Établissement à Paris d'une Banque Générale et Royale semblable à celle d'Amsterdam . . .," *Correspondance des Contrôleurs Généraux des Finances,* ed. De Boislisle, III, 641.

the Hoeuffts for France; the Huguetans, of Genevan origin, one of whom after lively adventures in French finance in this century, retired to Denmark and a second chapter of lively adventure; Hendrik Tersmitten, once a leading spirit of Colbert's Cie. du Nord; Benjamin Raulé, economic adviser to the Great Elector; Johan Deutz, factor for the sale of the emperor's quicksilver and *ipso facto* banker to that court; Balthazar Coymans of widespread commercial and financial interests, notably in Spain. The list could be greatly extended.[11]

The reputation of the bank was, as Sir William Temple said, " another invitation for People to come, and lodge here what part of their Money they could transport, and knew no way of securing at home. Nor did those People only lodge Moneys here, who came over into the Country; but many more, who never left their own; Though they provided for a retreat, or against a storm, and thought no place so secure as this, nor from whence they might so easily draw their Money into any parts of the World." [12]   In 1652 the Venetian secretary in London picked up a rumor that certain members of the Commonwealth parliament had " provided for a retreat " by remitting large sums of money to Holland, and were therefore disconcerted at the prospect of war with the Dutch.[13]   In the crisis of 1688 the Earls of Danby and Shrewsbury were reported to have taken the precaution of lodging funds in the bank of Amsterdam.[14]   In Denmark the attractive power of the bank was being strongly felt in the late years of the century: " Here the Courtier buys no Land, but remits his Money to the Bank of Amsterdam, or of Hamburg. . . . Moreover the Cash of the Nation runs yearly out, by what the Officers of the Army, who are Forreigners, can clear; for all that they

---

[11] The names have been culled at random from the alphabetical register of depositors kept by the bank, one for each year. These are now in the Gemeente Oud-Archief, Amsterdam, A.W.B. 4.

[12] *Observations upon the United Provinces of the Netherlands,* ed. G. N. Clark, p. 133. Bishop Huet wrote in almost the same sense, but may have copied Temple. *Mémoires sur le Commerce des Hollandois, dans tous les États et Empires du Monde* . . . (Amsterdam, 1718), p. 29.

[13] *Calendar of State Papers . . . Venice, 1647-1652,* ed. Allen B. Hinds (London, 1927), pp. 259, 261.

[14] *Memoirs of Sir John Reresby . . .,* ed. Andrew Browning (Glasgow, 1936), p. 521; T. C. Nicholson and A. S. Turberville, *Charles Talbot, Duke of Shrewsbury* (Cambridge [Eng.], 1930), p. 27.

transport to other Countries; likewise by what divers of the Ministers of State can scrape together; since it is observed, that few or none of them purchase any Lands, but place their Money in the Banks of Amsterdam and Hamburg." [15] The number of foreign accounts was undoubtedly large, but they are difficult to identify, as in many—probably most—cases they were covered by the names of Amsterdam agents. The Prince Palatine may have had funds in the bank in 1628, the Duke of Lorraine in 1652, but we do not know under what names they stood in the ledgers.[16] We know that the republic of Venice had funds in the bank in 1670, these too under a private name.[17] Foreign ambassadors and purchasing agents who received monies from their governments by bills of exchange, probably kept them in the bank, and certain politico-fiscal transactions between states, for example, the subsidies payable by Spain to Sweden in fulfillment of the treaties of 1668, were cleared through the bank.[18]

At its foundation the bank had been required to carry on its business in the best and heaviest coins at their legal values. As much of the currency in general use was of foreign origin, and commonly of inferior weight or fineness, an *agio* or premium arose between 'bank money' and the so-called *courantgeld*. In the second half of the century the *agio* fluctuated between 4½ and 5 per cent, occasionally rising higher. It was quoted on the price lists of the Amsterdam bourse from 1648, and commodity prices on those lists were commonly stated in bank money from 1683.[19] Long before this latter date the coins

---

[15] Robert Molesworth, *An Account of Denmark, as it was in the Year 1692* (London, 1694), pp. 84, 119-120.

[16] *Epistolae Ho-Elianae; the Familiar Letters of James Howell*, ed. John Jacobs (2 vols., London, 1892), I, 221; *Fifth Report of the Royal Commission on Historical Manuscripts* (London, 1876), p. 192.

[17] Gemeente Oud-Archief, Amsterdam, Diplom. Missiven, Engeland 3, Coenrad van Beuningen, ambassador in London, to the Burgomasters and Vroedschap, July 19, 1670.

[18] E.g., the Danish envoy, Corfits Ulevelt, had an account in the bank in 1651-1652, and the emperor's representative, Cramprich, one in 1688. (*Ibid.*, A.W.B. 4, alphabetical register of depositors, nos. 19, 21, 93.) For the fact of Spanish subsidies being handled through the bank: *Notulen gehouden ter Vergadering der Staten van Holland in 1670 door Hans Bontemantel*, ed. C. G. Smit (Werken uitgegeven door het Historisch Genootschap, 3rd ser., no. 67, Utrecht, 1937), pp. 3-4 and note.

[19] On the *agio*: Van Dillen, *Bronnen tot de Geschiedenis der Wisselbanken*,

preferred as bank currency had vanished from circulation in the Netherlands, and bank money had become almost wholly a money of account. Certain of the old heavy coins, however, had achieved such popularity in other lands that they continued to be extensively minted and almost as extensively exported by merchants for use in trade.[20] Efforts of Stuart kings to stop the importation of Dutch dollars in Scotland met with failure.[21] Jacques Savary sadly admitted that they were indispensable for the northern trades.[22] In Russia customs duties could be paid in no other currency, and though English merchants after long protest were allowed the alternative of paying in roubles, merchants of other nationalities were still being compelled to pay in Dutch dollars in the late eighteenth century.[23] The lion

I, 166 ff., and his "The Bank of Amsterdam," *History of the Principal Public Banks*, pp. 87 ff.; Z. W. Sneller, *Rotterdams Bedrijfsleven*, pp. 128 ff. See also an interesting discussion of the origin and working of the *agio* by Adam Smith, *An Inquiry into the Nature and Causes of the Wealth of Nations*, ed. Edwin Cannan (Modern Library, New York, 1937), pp. 445 ff. As to the recording of the *agio* on the price-lists of the bourse, and the quotation of commodity prices in bank-money, see Posthumus, *Nederlandsche Prijsgeschiedenis*, I, lix-lx.

[20] Van Dillen, "The Bank of Amsterdam," *History*, p. 83; also his "Amsterdam Marché Mondial des Métaux Précieux au xviie et au xviiie siècle," *Revue Historique* (1926), CLII, 4; Sneller, *Rotterdams Bedrijfsleven*, p. 135. In 1654 the Masters General of the Mint asserted that "*De rijksdaalder en de leeuwendaalder worden bijna alleen nog als negotiepenningen gebruikt.*" (Van Dillen, *Bronnen tot de Geschiedenis der Wisselbanken*, I, 110.)

[21] In the *Register of the Privy Council of Scotland* there are frequent allusions to the circulation of Dutch dollars in Scotland in this century, and to efforts of the government to stop it. For the prohibition of 1631 and the resistance of owners of coal mines and salt pans whose best customers were Hollanders with dollars in their pockets—resistance before which the Council was powerless—see the *Register* for the years 1630-1632, ed. P. H. Brown, 2nd ser., vol. IV (Edinburgh, 1902), 301-302, 522-523, 555-556; *ibid., 1633-1635,* vol. V (1904), 190-191, 203, 240, 341-342. That Dutch coins were still current in Scotland in the second half of the century is attested by an entry of Jan. 14, 1670. *Ibid., 1669-1672,* ed. P. H. Brown, 3rd ser., vol. III (1910), p. 126.

[22] Jacques Savary, *Le Parfait négociant ou instruction generale pour ce qui regarde le commerce* (Paris, 1675), book ii, p. 82; [Huet], *Mémoires sur le Commerce des Hollandois . . .,* p. 66; Le Moine de l'Espine, *Le Négoce d'Amsterdam ou traité de sa banque* (Amsterdam, 1694), p. 111.

[23] On the handicap to English trade with Russia resulting from the compulsion to procure Dutch currency, see the protest of the Muscovy Company in its instructions to its agent, John Hebdon, Sept. 16, 1676. (Public Record Office, State Papers, foreign, Russia 3, f. 213.) That this requirement still prevailed in the late eighteenth century for all nations trading to Russia (except the English, who had been exempted by treaty in 1766) is stated by J. B.

dollar of Holland was highly prized in the scales of the Levant, and the silver ducatons in the trade of India. From about 1660 the English East India Company imported ducatons in quantity to send to India. By the end of the century it was buying seven to eight million florins' worth of them annually.[24]

A cardinal responsibility of the bank from its foundation had been to supply the mints with the monetary metals, and to this end it had been empowered to buy bullion and foreign coin. This commerce was gradually enlarged until the bank was sending only a relatively small part of its stock of gold and silver to the mints, and was trading with the remainder in competition with the mintmasters, and with private exchangers and speculators. In 1683 it was authorized to make advances on the security of gold and silver deposited, to amounts somewhat below their market values.[25] Since receipts for bullion so deposited were negotiable, this procedure released an additional supply of credit to Amsterdam's business, drew the monetary metals from other lands, and confirmed the city as center of a world trade in gold and silver, a primacy it was to enjoy during the first half of the eighteenth century. "In this connection," wrote the author of a "Mémoire touchant le Négoce et la Navigation des Hollandois" in 1699, "it may well be said that all forms of gold and silver, coined or uncoined, are throughout Holland a sort of commodity that rises and falls, there being no law which prohibits export, or compels persons to bring them to the mint to be received at such or such price for such or such fineness." [26]

It is possible that the rise of Amsterdam as bullion market owed much to war trade with Spain, and something to war loot. Thus in 1595, and in several subsequent years down to 1630, the Spanish government was obliged to authorize export of the precious metals in return for grain imports.[27] In 1628 oc-

Scherer, *Histoire Raisonnée du commerce de la Russie* (2 vols., Paris, 1788), I, 124-125.

[24] Van Dillen, "Amsterdam Marché Mondial," *Revue Historique,* CLII, 4. On the lion dollar in Mediterranean trade: Van Dillen, *Bronnen tot de Geschiedenis der Wisselbanken,* I, 77; and the article "Aslani," *Dictionnaire Universel de Commerce* (1723), I, 166.

[25] Van Dillen, "The Bank of Amsterdam," *History,* pp. 102 ff., and his "Amsterdam Marché Mondial," *Revue Historique,* CLII, 4.

[26] *Bijdragen en Mededeelingen* (1903), XXIV, 311-312. (Translation.)

[27] Earl J. Hamilton, *American Treasure and the Price Revolution in Spain, 1501-1650* (Cambridge [Mass.], 1934), p. 249, note.

curred the famous capture of the Spanish treasure fleet by Piet Heyn, which netted 177,537 lbs. weight of silver, besides jewels and valuable commodities, the total estimated to come to 11½ to 15 million florins.[28] More important than such occasional windfalls was the share of Dutch merchants in the new silver brought twice a year to Cadiz from the mines of Mexico and Peru, a share which represented in part the profits of trade with Spain and through Spain with the New World. Just what that share was from year to year we do not know. Only a few fragmentary estimates for non-consecutive years in the second half of the century have come to light. According to these the Dutch usually carried off from 15 to 25 per cent of the treasure brought by the galleons and the *flota*, their share sometimes exceeding, sometimes falling below the amounts claimed by France or Genoa; ordinarily exceeding the respective portions of English, Flemish, and Hanseatic merchants.[29] The eagerness exhibited on the Amsterdam bourse for news of the safe arrival of the treasure fleets was certainly not disinterested.[30]

But direct remissions of silver from the bar of Cadiz to Holland were only part of the story. There was also indirect remis-

---

[28] Diferee, p. 267.

[29] Sir George Downing reported to Clarendon in 1662 that at least a third of the treasure brought by the plate fleet in that year would be taken over by the Dutch. (Lister, III, 182.) For the years 1670, 1681, 1682, 1685, and 1698, there are estimates by French consuls and correspondents in Spain. (Albert Girard, *Le Commerce français à Seville et Cadix au Temps des Habsbourg* . . . [Bibliothèque de l'École des Hautes Études Hispaniques, no. xvii, Paris, 1932], pp. 445 ff.) Henri Sée has recorded an estimate for 1691 ("Esquisse de l'Histoire du Commerce français à Cadix et dans l'Amérique Espagnole au xviiie siècle," *Revue d'Histoire Moderne* [1928], III, 15.) Dr. van Dillen refers to an estimate made near the end of the century which assigned about one-half of the American silver to the Dutch. ("Amsterdam Marché Mondial," *Revue Historique*, CLII, 3.) But so high an estimate must include silver belonging to nationals of other states sent to the Netherlands on Dutch ships.

[30] In 1661 Admiral de Ruyter received orders to make certain that the Spanish treasure fleet, in whose cargoes Dutch merchants were deeply interested should not fall into Portuguese hands. (P. J. Blok, *Michiel Adriaanszoon de Ruyter* ['s-Gravenhage, 1928], p. 177.) In 1663 Sir George Downing, and in 1667 William Temple, mentioned the concern felt in Amsterdam for news of the arrival of the silver fleet in Spain. (Bodleian Library, Clarendon MS. 107, f. 45 v., Downing to Clarendon, Dec. 18 [old style], 1663; Public Record Office, State Papers, foreign, Flanders 37, f. 118, Temple to Secretary Arlington, Sept. 19/29, 1667.)

sion from countries whose nationals had shared in the treasure discharged at Cadiz—remissions in payment for services or commodity purchases, attracted by speculative possibilities, or merely in quest of security and freedom of disposition. One comes upon frequent references to movements of coin and bullion from other countries to Holland. Much of the silver thus imported, possibly as much as half, was foreign-owned, the property of Spaniards, Netherlanders of the southern provinces, French subjects in the border towns recently incorporated into France, English merchants intent on getting a better price for their silver.[31] Silver for the king of Spain was sent to Holland after the Peace of Westphalia with the stipulation that one third of such consignments might be sent to the mints while two thirds were to remain uncoined at the king's disposition.[32] An English merchant in Livorno in 1666 mentioned that a large part of the American silver shipped from Cadiz to Genoa and Livorno was the property of Dutch houses in those cities.[33] English and French writers in this century were prone to credit the Dutch with devilish ingenuity in drawing away their currencies by manipulation of exchange. Actually the Dutch experienced the monetary troubles endemic in this century, and before the reforms of the eighties and nineties were unable to prevent the deterioration of their own currency. The precious metals which flowed into Amsterdam so freely and briskly, flowed out again as freely and nearly as briskly. The mintmasters, especially in the second half of the century, kept up an almost continual outcry over the rising price of silver which they attributed to export of that metal, now to England, now to France, to the Spanish Netherlands, to Germany.[34] Silver for the imperial mints was bought in Amsterdam, although there was a considerable output of that metal from mines in Habsburg territories.[35] An intendant of French

---

[31] Van Dillen, "Amsterdam Marché Mondial," Revue Historique, CLII, 3; Gerard Malynes, The Maintenance of Free Trade (London, 1622), pp. 11-12.

[32] Van Dillen, Bronnen tot de Geschiedenis der Wisselbanken, I, 96-97. Prior to that peace silver destined for Amsterdam was consigned via Hamburg. Ibid., I, 76-77.

[33] Public Record Office, State Papers, foreign, Tuscany 6, Charles Chillingworth to Joseph Williamson, Dec. 23/Jan. 2, 1665/6.

[34] Van Dillen, Bronnen tot de Geschiedenis der Wisselbanken, I, 102, 109-110, 135, 196, 216 ff.

[35] Srbik, pp. 72-73.

Flanders in 1707 observed with gratification the flow of coin from Holland through the Spanish provinces and so into France, to the tune of more than a million livres a month.[36] Trade with northern and Baltic countries, with Mediterranean lands, and with the East, called forth a heavy export of silver in coin or plate.[37] Ultimately this export was compensated by import, especially, as we have seen, in the trade with Spain, but also in consequence of invisible items in the balance of trade such as freight charges, brokers' commissions, payments for lighterage, storage, and transit facilities; for banking, exchange, and insurance services; for building or chartering ships, and provisioning, arming, and paying troops; remittances from Dutchmen gainfully employed in trade or other capacities abroad; returns from foreign capital operating in the Netherlands, and from Dutch capital invested in foreign lands.[38] In 1683 the mintmasters informed the States General that the normal annual importation of silver might range from 15 to 18 million florins, and of this about 13 million might be carried out again.[39]

When the broadest allowance has been made for the monetary requirements of trade in causing an ebb and flow of precious metals between country and country, it remains

---

[36] *Correspondance des Contrôleurs Généraux des Finances . . .*, ed. De Boislisle, II, 400-401. In 1668 the deputies of the province of Zeeland had informed the States General that the silver coin of the republic was being transported in great quantity to France and there recoined. Rijks Archief, Resolutiën Staten Generaal, July 30, 1668.

[37] "Every one knows that Norway, the East-Country, Smyrna, Persia, India, China, &c. do afford us infinitely more Merchandize than they take of us, we cannot trade with them but by Gold and Silver; and that moreover, these Provinces, at least that of Holland, cannot subsist without the said Traffick." [La Court], *True Interest*, p. 98. For a similar argument: Van Dillen, *Bronnen tot de Geschiedenis der Wisselbanken*, I, 220-221.

[38] In 1646 Jean Eon mentioned by name a number of Dutch merchants who, after building up large fortunes in the trade of Nantes, retired to the Netherlands with their capital. Similar withdrawals, he declared, had taken place in other French trading cities. (*Le Commerce Honorable . . . composé par un Habitant de la Ville de Nantes* [Nantes, 1646], pp. 103-104.) More general charges of this nature by French and English writers were not uncommon in this century. We have already glanced at the role of foreign capital in the rise of Amsterdam (above, pp. 23-24) and shall have more to say on the investment of Amsterdam capital in foreign countries. (Below, pp. 104 ff.)

[39] Van Dillen, *Bronnen tot de Geschiedenis der Wisselbanken*, I, 220-221.

probable that this restless movement was strongly influenced by speculation. The competition of mints for the monetary metals, defects in minting techniques which resulted in inequalities of weight in coins of the same nominal value, the appreciating value of gold in terms of silver, and sudden fluctuations in prices when the silver fleets were reported at Cadiz, or East India fleets sailed from Texel or Thames carrying off much silver in their holds—all this made speculation in the precious metals a tempting, though a hazardous business. Amsterdam was the natural seat of such trading, not only because of advantages already described, but also because the world's news came to her door, and traders in bullion could act on the best information then available. The ratio of silver to gold in Holland influenced strongly the currency situation in both England and France in this century. Efforts of James I's government to check the export of coin to the Netherlands may have contributed to the currency crisis of 1621.[40] In the middle years of the century English gold abounded in Amsterdam,[41] and in the last quarter the operation of the Dutch ratio was sweeping England clean of her silver and substituting gold.[42]

Freedom to export the monetary metals, rare elsewhere in the seventeenth century, helped to stabilize exchange rates in Amsterdam [43] and so encouraged the circulation of bills of exchange as negotiable instruments of credit, the discounting and sale of which became a lively business in the city. In the trade of no other country in this period, except the experienced Italian cities, now well past the meridian of their commercial grandeur, was the bill of exchange used so freely and

[40] Below, p. 123. On the gravitation of English coin to Holland in the first quarter of the century: E. Lipson, *The Economic History of England* (3 vols., London, 1931-1937), III, 74, 78; Tobias Gentleman, "England's Way to win Wealth," *The Harleian Miscellany* (12 vols., London, 1808-1811), III, 238; *Calendar of Treasury Books*, 1695-1702, ed. W. A. Shaw (London, 1934), p. cviii.

[41] Lipson, III, 90.

[42] *Calendar of Treasury Books, 1695-1702*, introduction, pp. cix ff. The English East India Company was suspected of smuggling English coin over to Holland, whence its equivalent would be returned, when return was advantageous, in the guise of foreign bullion. (Lipson, II, 280.)

[43] Van Dillen, "Amsterdam Marché Mondial," *Revue Historique*, CLII, 5; Sayous, "Le Rôle d'Amsterdam dans l'histoire du capitalisme," *ibid.*, CLXXXIII, 263.

flexibly, and no other city in this century had a business in them equal to Amsterdam's. Neither French, Spanish, Scottish, nor Italian cities could provide direct and current exchange with northern and northeastern Europe, and London was in little better case; hence exchange to and from these countries flowed through Amsterdam, with a smaller stream through Hamburg.[44] Exchange from Lisbon, when Savary wrote, seems to have been a practical monopoly of the correspondents of Amsterdam houses.[45] If it were not strictly true that Amsterdam was *"le théâtre ou tous les changes du monde se font,"* as a member of the French Council of Commerce asserted in 1700, this was an exaggeration along the line of the facts.[46] Exchange rates on the principal cities to which Amsterdam traded were quoted on the price lists of the bourse. The earliest printed list extant, that of 1585, shows that Amsterdam had then established exchange relations with ten cities, a number which gradually increased. The lists do not, however, afford a complete picture of the net of exchanges of which Amsterdam was the center. Exchange could be arranged there on almost any town having trade, but for less frequented places, as Vienna or Algiers, rates were apt to be high.[47]

Familiarity with the bill of exchange not only in settling commercial balances between one place and another, but also

[44] " Il faut observer qu'il n'y a que deux endroits où l'on puisse avoir correspondance pour envoyer de l'argent dans toutes les villes du Nort, & pour y faire les traites, & remises, qui sont Amsterdam, & Hambourg." Savary, book ii, p. 86. On the limited exchange relations of London when Lewes Roberts wrote *The Merchants Mappe of Commerce* (London, 1638), see part ii, p. 256 of that edition.

[45] Savary, book ii, p. 81.

[46] " Extrait du mémoire du Sieur des Casaux, député de Nantes . . ." in Germain Martin's *La Grande Industrie sous le règne de Louis XIV* (Paris, 1898), p. 396.

[47] Posthumus, I, 579 ff. In 1734 rates of exchange on some 25 cities were being quoted on the price-lists of the Amsterdam bourse. (*Ibid.*, I, 581.) Le Moine de l'Espine distinguished between the cities with which Amsterdam maintained *change ouvert,* and those not in this category. Of the latter he wrote: " On y pourroit même trouver dans le besoin des lettres pour Coppenhague en Dannemarck; pour Stockholme en Suede; pour Riga, Lubec, Archangel en Moskovie & pour Smyrne & Alep dans le Levant, quoi qu'il n'y ait point de change ordinaire pour ces Places." (*Le Négoce d'Amsterdam* [1694], pp. 11-12.) In the exchange from Amsterdam on Vienna could be transacted only at a premium ranging from 5½ to 11 per cent. (Srbik, p. 31.) The premium on exchange from Amsterdam on Algiers in 1680 came to 30 per cent. (Rijks Archief, Resolutiën Staten Generaal, Feb. 14, 1681.)

as a means of anticipating credits, may have encouraged acceptance of other forms of paper credit current in Amsterdam: merchants' notes, receipts for bullion deposited in the bank, or for merchandise stored in warehouses, debentures of the India companies, municipal bonds—all these passing freely from hand to hand constituted an expanding fund of credit which made Amsterdam less dependent on hard money than were other trading cities of northern Europe. This was illustrated in 1650 when the Prince of Orange was endeavoring to borrow £20,000 in cash for the exiled Charles II. Time passed, and Charles's advisers became anxious.

The prince told them, that he believed that they who knew London so well, and had heard so much discourse of the wealth of Holland, would wonder very much that he should have been endeavouring above ten days to borrow twenty thousand pounds; and that the richest men in Amsterdam had promised to supply him with it, and that one half of it was not yet provided. He said, it was not that there was any question of his credit, which was very good; and that the security he gave was as good as any body desired, and upon which he could have double the sum in less time if he would receive it in paper, which was the course of that country; and where, bargains being made for one hundred thousand pounds to be paid within ten days, it was never known that twenty thousand pounds was paid together in one town, but by bills upon Rotterdam, Harlem, the Hague, and Antwerp, and other places, which was as convenient, or more, to all parties; and he did verily believe that though Amsterdam could pay a million within a month upon any good occasion, that yet they would be troubled to bring twenty thousand pounds together into any one room; and that was the true reason that the money was not yet brought to the Hague, which it should be within few days; as it was accordingly.[48]

The prince's explanation is a reminder that the long arm of Amsterdam capitalism which reached to foreign lands, drew

[48] Clarendon, *The History of the Rebellion and Civil Wars in England,* V, 48. Other English writers contrasted the easy credit conditions prevailing in Holland, with the close dependence of English trade on hard money: Andrew Yarranton, *England's Improvement by Sea and Land . . .* (London, 1677), pp. 7, 141; John Collins, *A Plea for the bringing in of Irish Cattle* (London, 1680), pp. 16-17; Josiah Child, *A New Discourse of Trade* (2d ed., London, 1694), pp. 6-7. Although assignment of bills of debt was legalized in England in 1698 (9-10 W. 3, c. 17), they had little circulation in Queen Anne's reign. *Defoe's Review 1704-1713 reproduced from the original edition by A. W. Secord* (Facsimile Text Society, 22 vols., New York, 1938), VI, 23, 149.

also on the capital and resources of neighbor towns in the United Provinces. Other cities of Holland and Zeeland with a will to autonomy as jealous as Amsterdam's own, resisted to the best of their abilities economic dependence on the metropolis. They had their chambers in the India companies; they founded exchanges, banks, courts of assurance. But these institutions were enfeebled by the accessibility and superior business opportunities of the greater market. Some of their industries were either penetrated directly by Amsterdam capitalism, or subordinated to the demands of the export trade centered there.[49] Beyond the confines of the United Provinces, the Hanseatic cities of the ' little East ' found themselves reduced to the position of satellites of Amsterdam, and westward the attraction of the metropolis was felt in the southern Netherlands and northern France.

In the more spacious orbit of Amsterdam's financial and business relationships most of commercial Europe was eventually included. Italian exchangers had appeared in Amsterdam in the late sixteenth century.[50] Antwerp capital, diminished as

[49] For the influence of Amsterdam capital on the industries of other Dutch towns, see pp. 72-73, below. The exchange bank of Rotterdam was established in 1635 to meet the needs of the Merchant Adventurers whose court had been moved to that city. In practice it proved impossible for the Rotterdam bank to furnish exchange on London to the amounts required by the one-way trade of the Fellowship. Instead, the Merchant Adventurers received their Rotterdam credits in bills of exchange on Amsterdam, from which city they could be easily relayed to London. (Sneller, " De Rotterdamsche Wisselbank," *Rotterdams Bedrijfsleven*, pp. 115-116, 141 ff., 155-156.) Sir William Brereton, visiting Rotterdam in 1634, thought the bourse insignificant. (*Travels in Holland the United Provinces England Scotland and Ireland 1634-1635*, ed. Edward Hawkins [Chetham Society Publications, vol. I, London, 1844], p. 11.) In Rotterdam there was little or no speculative trading in the actions of the local chamber of the India companies (see below, p. 77) nor do we hear of rings of merchant capitalists there attempting to corner available supplies of important commodities. (Elzinga, p. 162.) Since Rotterdam's wealth was unquestionably increasing in this century, it would seem probable that a good part of the surplus not required for her trade, found its way to Amsterdam for investment.

[50] They are mentioned in a letter of 1596. (*Calendar of the Manuscripts of . . . the Marquis of Salisbury . . . at Hatfield House . . .* [Royal Commission on Historical Manuscripts], Part VI [London, 1895], p. 499.) When Giorgio Giustiniano visited Amsterdam in 1608, he found the merchant and banking house of the Calandrini already established there. (*Relazioni Veneziane. Venetiaansche Berichten over de Vereenigde Nederlanden van 1600-1795*, ed. P. J. Blok [Rijks Geschiedkundige Publicatiën, no. 7, 's-Gravenhage, 1909], p. 15.)

it was after the recovery of that city by Spain, was found buying shares in the East India Company in 1608.[51] Venetians and French invested in the West Indian Company.[52] Florentines had banks in the city in the mid-century, and there were Tuscan shareholders in the East India Company.[53] A company of Genoese merchants had a ship built in Amsterdam with which they traded to Portugal, Spain, and the Mediterranean.[54] A colony of Armenians imported silks from Russia, Turkey, Persia, and India.[55] Von Zesen has drawn a lively picture of the bourse at the rush hour between noon and one o'clock, when Germans, Poles, Hungarians, Walloons, Frenchmen, Spaniards, Russians, Turks — " yes, at times Hindus and other foreign peoples "— shouldered one another in a polylingual hubbub of bargaining.[56]

Because much of the capital active in Amsterdam was foreign-owned or owned by Amsterdammers of foreign birth, and much Dutch-owned capital was not fixed in land, houses, or industrial plant, but in assets easily liquidated or transferred, it was peculiarly sensitive and mobile. The shocks of the English and French wars demonstrated this mobility. In 1672 when the French invasion threatened the city, wealth sought safety in flight. Prudent Florentines had withdrawn their funds as early as February.[57] In June the flight of capital became

---

[51] *Calendar of State Papers . . . Venice, 1607-1610,* ed. Horatio F. Brown (London, 1904), p. 144.

[52] *Piet Heyn en de Zilver Vloot,* eds. S. P. Honoré Naber and Irene A. Wright (Werken uitgegeven door het Historisch Genootschap, 3rd ser., no. 53, Utrecht, 1928), p. lvi.

[53] The sympathy manifested by Florentines for the Dutch in the second Anglo-Dutch war was attributed by Sir John Finch, the English resident, to " their particular dependence upon Amsterdam diverse of them having banckes in Amsterdam; and I believe many more concern'd in the Dutch East India Company." (Public Record Office, State Papers, foreign, Tuscany 5, Sir John Finch to Secretary Arlington, Oct. 10/20, 1665.) An Italian traveller in 1677 had letters of exchange on Gioacchino Guasconi and H. da Verrazano, " *gentiluomo fiorentino,*" of Amsterdam. ("Een Italiaansche Reisbeschrijving der Nederlanden [1677-1678]," ed. Gisbert Brom, *Bijdragen en Mededeelingen* [1915], XXXVI, 106.)

[54] *Calendar of State Papers, domestic series, 1666-1667,* ed. M. A. E. Green (London, 1864), p. 83.

[55] Diferee, p. 161.

[56] Filips von Zesen, *Beschreibung der Stadt Amsterdam* (Amsterdam, 1664), pp. 232-233. (Translation.)

[57] *Calendar of State Papers . . . Venice, 1671-1672,* ed. Allen B. Hinds (London, 1939), p. 170.

panic. "Within these 3 or 4 dayes above 10 millions of gilders in money and gold have been conveyed from the Hague to Amsterdam, and all the Jewes and Rich Marchants drawes all the Money they can out of Amsterdam upon Venice Legorne and other places, the Exchange from Amsterdam upon Venice was the last Post at 105 pence for a Ducat, having been the Weeke before at 85." [58] "You may easily believe," wrote an Englishman from Brussels, "that they are in a desperate condition when they doe at this time give from 10 to 17 per cent. to have bills for Antwerp or any of these Countrys for monies, as quite despairing of their own." [59] On the same day the Venetian secretary in London informed the Senate that "the exchange on Holland is 16 per cent. in favour of London; and it appeares to me, that a number of rich Dutch families purpose to come hither, while some have gone to Hamburg, and all are intent on preserving their private property." [60] Bonds of the province of Holland sank to 30 per cent of their par value, and East India shares were thrown on the market at half their pre-war price.[61] The bank of Amsterdam rode out the crisis, as we have seen, thanks to its large reserves of gold and silver, and to prompt action on the part of the municipal government.[62] Similar though less sharp visitations of financial panic occurred in 1675, 1681, and 1710.[63]

But these crises were of short duration. Not all capital

[58] Public Record Office, State Papers, foreign, Flanders 40, f. 140, James Nipho, Antwerp, to Joseph Williamson, June 8/18, 1672 (copy).

[59] *Ibid.*, Flanders 40, f. 152, R. Bulstrode to [S. Cottington?], June 14/24, 1672.

[60] *Calendar of State Papers . . . Venice, 1671-1672*, pp. 230-231.

[61] H. Brugmans, "Handel en Nijverheid," *Amsterdam in de Zeventiende Eeuw*, II, 40; J. Grossmann, *Die Amsterdamer Börse voor 200 Jahren* (Den Haag, 1876), pp. 15 ff., 111-112; Z. W. Sneller, *Economische Crisissen in Vroeger Tijd* (Kampen, 1932), p. 11.

[62] See above, p. 44.

[63] The panic of 1675 was set off by a rumor that acceptance of the title of Duke of Gelders by William III would serve as a test of public support for conversion of the republic into a monarchy. (*Letters written by Sir William Temple . . .* [3 vols., London, 1700-1701], III, pp. 146-147.) In October 1681, rumor of an alliance with Sweden precipitated a war scare. (P. de Ségur-Dupeyron, *Histoire des négociations commerciales et maritimes de la France au xviie et xviiie siècles* [3 vols., Paris, 1872-1873], II, 64.) The break in 1710 was occasioned by the failure of peace negotiations at Gertruidenburg, the fall of the Whig ministry in England, and the death of the emperor. (Srbik, p. 312.)

ran away, and much that ran, returned when assured of safety. Dutch public finance was strained to the utmost in the struggle against Louis XIV, but though the poor, taxed to the bone, were probably growing poorer, it is apparent that the rich were growing richer. The pre-eminence of Amsterdam as market for capital was to become still stronger in the eighteenth century.[64]

[64] See the opinion of Charles Davenant in 1698: *The Political and Commercial Works . . . of Charles D'Avenant,* ed. Sir Charles Whitworth (5 vols., London, 1771), I, 352. Also, the opinion of Adam Smith more than a century later: *An Inquiry into . . . the Wealth of Nations,* ed. Cannan, p. 91. A very general idea of the growth of Amsterdam's wealth may be gained from the increased yield of taxes on property, real and personal, levied in 1585, 1631, 1674, and 1742, but as the bases of assessment for these levies differed considerably, no accurate comparison can be made. Van Dillen, *Amsterdam in 1585;* and by the same, *Bedrijfsleven,* II, xxxvi ff.; G. W. Kernkamp, "Amsterdam Patriciërs," *Vragen des Tijds* (1905), XXXII, 20 ff., 33 ff.; Charles Wilson, *Anglo-Dutch Commerce and Finance in the eighteenth century* (Cambridge [Eng.], 1941), pp. 16 ff.

CHAPTER III

PUBLIC IMPROVEMENTS—INVESTMENT IN LAND AND INDUSTRY

The concentration of capital in Amsterdam in this century was great for the time, and would surely have produced catastrophic inflation if this capital had not been drawn off in enterprises both public and private. Port improvements were undertaken on a generous scale.[1] In the middle decades of the century the enlargement and embellishment of Amsterdam called for a heavy investment alike of public and private funds. Sir William Temple has described the ' New Town ' which then came into being: " The Extent whereof is so spacious, and the Buildings of so much greater Beauty and Cost than the Old, that it must have employ'd a vast proportion of that Stock which in this City was before wholly turned into Trade." [2] Each of the twenty-two bastions built for the defense of the enlarged city was reported to have cost f. 500,000, and the new and magnificent *stadhuis*, today a palace, cost f. 7,825,000.[3] In 1662 the city was paying out f. 1,441,000 for public works, but this sum was to be drastically cut during the period of the French wars.[4] Von Zesen has described with ecstatic admiration the splendid houses of merchant princes on the Keizersgracht, adorned with works of art and luxury from the four quarters of the world.[5]

During the first half of the century much capital was invested in land, especially in polder enterprises in the vicinity of Amsterdam, elsewhere in Holland, and in other provinces.

[1] Jan Wagenaar, *Amsterdam in zyne Opkomst, Aanwas, Geschiedenissen . . . beschreven* (3 vols., Amsterdam, 1760-1767), III, 65.

[2] *Observations upon the United Provinces of the Netherlands,* ed. Clark, p. 150.

[3] " Drie Brieven van Samuel Sorbière over den Toestand van Holland in 1660," communicated by P. J. Blok, *Bijdragen en Mededeelingen* (1901), XXII, 18; H. J. Koenen, *Voorlezingen over de Geschiedenis der Finantiën van Amsterdam* (Amsterdam, 1855), p. 24.

[4] H. S. M. van Wickevoort Crommelin, " Hoe Amsterdam aan Geld kwam," *De Economist* (1898), XLVII, 909.

[5] *Beschreibung der Stadt Amsterdam*, pp. 357-358.

Between 1597 and 1635 the Zijpe and Wieringerwaard were diked in, the Beemster, Zoetermeer, Purmer, 's-Gravenland and several smaller meres were drained. Although the capital of other towns was enlisted for these undertakings, the leading role was Amsterdam's.[6] In the Zijpe Amsterdam capital had been interested from the inception of the project, but between 1596 and 1619 the number of Amsterdam proprietors in that polder rose from nineteen to forty-four. Their names and wealth suggest that urban capital had been attracted to this strip of marshy coast by the rise of rental values in the densely populated province of Holland.[7]

A part of the new wealth found its way into industry. Amsterdam was never to become an industrial city like Leiden or Haarlem, but in the seventeenth century her industry took on a cosmopolitan and competitive character strongly influenced by her foreign trade.[8] An important group of industries was concerned with finishing or refining commodities imported in a crude or partly manufactured state: the dyeing and finishing of English cloth and says; dressing leathers as chamois or

[6] G. W. Kernkamp, " Amsterdam Patriciërs," *Vragen des Tijds*, XXXII, 27 ff. There are diagrams of these polders in *L'Atlas de Gerard Mercator et d'Hondius* (1633), I, 377 f. Brief mention of the Beemster was made in note 52, p. 28, above. See also the description by Sir William Temple, *Observations*, pp. 93-94. For a full history of the undertaking, see J. Bouman, *Bedijking, Opkomst en Bloei van de Beemster*.

[7] J. Belonje, " Amsterdamsch Grondbezit in de Zijpe," *Jaarboek Amstelodamum*, XXXIII, 37 ff. On the cost to the public of maintaining the land by dikes and drainage, see [La Court], *True Interest*, pp. 21-22; Temple, p. 95.

[8] On Amsterdam's industrial development in this period, see H. Brugmans, " Handel en Nijverheid," *Amsterdam in de Zeventiende Eeuw*, II, 197 ff., and the two volumes of sources edited by J. G. van Dillen, *Bronnen tot de Geschiedenis van het Bedrijfsleven en het Gildewezen*, particularly the introductions. This collection extends at present only to the year 1632. For the city's industries in the late years of the century, one may consult Le Moine de l'Espine, *Le Négoce d'Amsterdam*, pp. 42-43; and [Huet], *Mémoires sur le commerce des Hollandois*, pp. 32-33. The introduction of certain crafts from the southern provinces in the late sixteenth and early seventeenth centuries has been touched upon, above, p. 24. Those represented in the French immigration in the late decades of the seventeenth century may be inferred from "Stukken betreffende de Nijverheid der Refugiés te Amsterdam," ed. Leonie van Nierop, *Economisch-historisch Jaarboek* (1921), VII, 147 ff.; *ibid.*, (1923), IX, 157 ff. Interesting sidelights on Amsterdam industry have been gleaned by Dr. van Nierop from advertisements appearing in Amsterdam newspapers in the second half of the seventeenth century. "Gegevens over de Nijverheid van Amsterdam bijeengelezen uit de advertenties in de *Amsterdamsche Courant* 1667-1794," *Jaarboek Amstelodamum* (1930), XXVII, 261 ff.

morocco, or carving and gilding them; the processing and dye-ing of silk yarns; the bleaching of wax and refining of oils, dyes, and drugs; the use of oriental woods and lacquers in cabinet-making; the printing of East-India calicoes. The com-ing of over four hundred silk workers from Antwerp and other towns of the southern Netherlands in the years 1585-1606, and the new sea-borne trade with Italy and the East Indies, the countries producing raw silk, drew the attention of Amsterdam-mers to the possibilities of an industry which should include the weaving of broad silks as well as the dyeing and processing of silk yarns. In 1605 five prominent merchants of the city con-cluded a contract with the East India Company by which the Company was to furnish supplies of raw silk at a fixed price, and the merchants engaged to have the silk manufactured in Amsterdam.[9] We are not informed of the outcome of this particular enterprise, but before the mid-century the industry was well established, and in the second half of the century Amsterdam silks could compete in European markets with those of Lyon and Tours. Certain Amsterdam textiles seem to have been almost too French to be admitted without suspic-ion by English customs officers after the ban imposed on French manufactures; others were almost too Indian.[10]

Sugar-refining, also introduced from Antwerp in the late sixteenth century, became Amsterdam's leading industry, hav-ing about fifty bakeries in 1662, in which Portuguese residents had made substantial investment.[11] Tobacco cutting and wrap-

---

[9] Leonie van Nierop, " De Zijdenijverheid van Amsterdam," *Tijdschrift voor Geschiedenis* (1930), XLV, 18 ff., 151 ff.; Van Dillen, *Bedrijfsleven*, I, 622.

[10] According to Le Moine de l'Espine Amsterdam produced brocades and silks *" plus belles et riches que dans les autres Villes, & qui diffèrent peu de celles de France, & reviennent à 15 ou 20. p.c. moins."* (*Le Négoce d'Amster-dam*, p. 42.) A French *mémoire* of 1686 declared that the silk brocades of Lyon and Tours were no longer in the same demand in Spain and the Indies, *" Depuis quelques années, la concurrence hollandaise a tué cette exportation. Les marchands français se fournissent en Hollande."* On the last galleons and the *flota* Hollanders had shipped gold and silver brocades to the value of a million livres. (Girard, pp. 367-368.) On the difficulties of English customs offi-cials in distinguishing Dutch silks from the French and Indian fabrics which they imitated: Charles Davenant, *Works*, I, 108-109; *Calendar of State Papers, domestic series, 1699-1700*, ed. Edward Bateson (London, 1937), p. 31.

[11] J. J. Reesse, *De Suikerhandel van Amsterdam van het Begin der 17de Eeuw tot 1813* . . . (Haarlem, 1908), pp. 105 ff., 127 ff.; Van Dillen, *Bedrijfsleven*, I, 504, and frequent mention of sugár-bakers and sugar-baking thereafter; M.

ping consumed quantities of English and French colonial leaf, as well as that grown in the Netherlands.[12] Even French wines underwent 'sophistication,' and Colbert was perturbed by the suspicion that they might be preferred so in northern countries.[13] The distilling of brandy, an outgrowth of the wine trade, attained some importance in Amsterdam in the second half of the century.[14] Although Dordrecht and some smaller towns excelled the metropolis in salt-boiling and refining, Amsterdam had 32 pans in the middle of the century.[15]

In the cutting and polishing of lenses for spectacles, telescopes, etc., and in the manufacture of mathematical and scientific instruments, Amsterdam enjoyed a European reputation, though it is not now possible to distinguish her achievement in this field from that of Rotterdam or Leiden, much of whose output was probably sold in Amsterdam. In the eighteenth century Amsterdam was still the place to come to for instruments of precision: " There is a greater Choice of Astrono-

---

Fokkens, *Beschrijvinge der wijdt-vermaarde Koopstadt Amstelredam* . . . (Amsterdam, 1662), p. 354; Von Zesen, pp. 90, 371. In the only surviving list of imports and exports passing through the port of Amsterdam in this century, that for the year 1667-1668, we find the following data:

	Imports	Exports
Molasses	2,234 pipes	159,8 pipes
Sugar, white and muscovado	1,028,520 lbs.	425,210 lbs.
Sugar, panel	6,213,610 lbs.	208,065 lbs.
Sugar, broad and banquet	1,700 lbs.	1,727,729 lbs.

(H. Brugmans, "Statistiek van den In- en Uitvoer van Amsterdam, 1 October 1667-30 September 1668," *Bijdragen en Mededeelingen* [1898], XIX, pp. 173, 175.) For the importance of the Dutch market to the export trade in raw sugars from the English and French West Indian islands, see below pp. 93, 95.

[12] A company for spinning and wrapping tobacco was formed in Amsterdam in 1631. (Van Dillen, *Bedrijfsleven*, II, 759.) On the development of this industry: Brugmans, "Handel en Nijverheid," *Amsterdam in de Zeventiende Eeuw* II, 208-209; Van Dillen, "De Economische Positie en Betekenis der Joden," *Geschiedenis*, I, pp. 572 ff. Tobacco imported at Amsterdam in 1667-1668 was valued at f. 271,467; that exported at f. 526,736. (Brugmans, "Statistiek . . .," *Bijdragen*, XIX, 176.) On the Dutch market for English and French West Indian tobacco, see below, p. 93, n. 33.

[13] Mathorez, II, 246; Van Dillen, *Bedrijfsleven*, II, p. xxiv; Cole, I, 413.

[14] Brugmans, "Handel en Nijverheid," *Amsterdam . . .*, II, 210; Van Dillen, *Bedrijfsleven*, II, xxx.

[15] "Memorie wegens het Verval van de Soutkeeten tot Amsterdam" [1736?] (Gemeente Oud-Archief, Amsterdam, Arch. Burg., Portefeuille Handel 11). By 1670, or a year not far from that date the number of pans had declined to 22. "Memorij wat keeten, en hoe veel pannen hier sijn soo in Hollandt, Seelandt, de Maes, en Frieslant," *ibid*.

mical, Geometrical, and other Mathematical Instruments in Holland, than any where else in the World." [16]   The manufacture of munitions, developing out of the trade in that merchandise, grew rapidly during the second half of the century, Hamburg being eclipsed in this respect as she had earlier been eclipsed in the trade.[17] Dutch gunfounders, as we have seen, were reputed "the most expert founders in the World," and Pieter Marcelis shipped the guns cast in his new Russian foundry all the way to Holland to be bored.[18]

Type-casting and printing were export industries in Amsterdam. The types used by Dutch printers in the first half of the century were derived from French designs and from German punches, but from the mid-century printers were also using types originated by distinguished Amsterdam type-founders, Christoffels van Dijk and the brothers Voskens. Dutch types, whether designed at home or abroad, acquired an international reputation through the popularity of works issued in cheap and convenient format by the Elzevir press, those "bookes of an Amsterdam print" bought by Thomas Hobbes to carry in his pocket and read in antechambers while his lord, the duke of Devonshire, was paying visits.[19] Dutch types were much copied abroad, and punches and matrices as well as types were exported. In England, where type-founding was discouraged by Star Chamber in 1637, Dutch founts were in common use. The press presented to Oxford University by Dr. John Fell, and the first presses in use in England's American colonies, were furnished with types purchased in Holland.[20]   "There was

[16] *A Description of Holland: or the Present State of the United Provinces* (1743), p. 236. Crystal glass-blowing had been initiated in Amsterdam early in the seventeenth century. (Van Dillen, *Bedrijfsleven*, I, 548-549.)

[17] E. Baasch, "Der Verkehr mit Kriegsmaterialen aus und nach den Hansestädten," *Jahrbücher für Nationalökonomie und Statistik* (1932), CXXXVII, 543. See the figures for Amsterdam's imports and exports of munitions for the year 1667-1668, Brugman's "Statistiek," *Bijdragen*, XIX, p. 133.

[18] P. 41, above; Scheltema, *Rusland en de Nederlanden*, I, 230.

[19] Ch. Enschedé, *Fonderies de caractères et leur matériel dans les pays-bas du xve au xixe siècle . . .* (Haarlem, 1908), pp. 34-111. A. F. Johnson, *Type Designs: their history and development* (London, 1934), pp. 66 ff., 71-72, 80 ff., 160; Alphonse Willems, *Les Elzeviers histoire et annales typographiques* (2 vols., Bruxelles, 1880); John Aubrey, '*Brief Lives*' *chiefly of Contemporaries,* ed. Andrew Clark (Oxford, 1898, 2 vols.), I, 331.

[20] Johnson, pp. 68 ff.; Lawrence C. Wroth, *The Colonial Printer* (Portland [Maine], 1938), p. 87; George Parker Winship, *The Cambridge Press, 1638-*

half of the century Dutch gazettes were relied on by London-ers for continental news.[30] Bulstrode Whitelocke found them circulating in Sweden, and recently an extraordinary collection of 1,300 numbers of 15 different *corantos*, published for the most part in Amsterdam in the years 1618-1665, has been dis-covered in Stockholm.[31]

From what has been said of Amsterdam's industrial develop-ment in this century it is evident that much of the initiative and presumably much of the capital was supplied by mer-chants. Naturalization of a manufacture based on foreign models and often requiring a formidable outlay in plant and tools, imported raw materials and, in some cases, imported skills, demanded not only capital and organizing ability, but a competent knowledge of foreign industry and foreign markets. Dutch historians have drawn a distinction between such com-mercial industries (*verkeersindustriën*) which developed in a few trading towns, notably Amsterdam, and manufactories (*fabrieken*) of an older type found in Leiden and other in-dustrial cities. The former worked up imported materials for foreign markets; their prime requisite was capital, and hand-craftsmanship played a secondary role. The *fabrieken*, on the other hand, depended on a complicated integration of skilled crafts, which made wages a prime consideration, while capital for plant, equipment, and marketing had less significance.[32] The distinction is suggestive, though it cannot be applied without qualification to industries in Amsterdam or elsewhere at this time. Certain of the city's industries which have just

Amsterdam, the Hague, and elsewhere in Holland, all antedate the London *Weekly Newes*, long considered the earliest printed English newspaper.

[30] E.g., Charles II and the Duke of York found the *Haarlem Gazette* rather too well-informed about what was going on in England. (*The Diary of Samuel Pepys* . . ., ed. Henry B. Wheatley with Lord Braybrooke's notes [9 vols., London, 1893-1899], VI, 223, March 24, 1666/67.) Robert Hooke, the scientist, read a Dutch gazette in London. (*The Diary of Robert Hooke 1672-1680*, eds. H. W. Robinson and Walter Adams [London, 1935], p. 23.)

[31] Bulstrode Whitelocke, *A Journal of the Swedish Embassy in the Years 1653 and 1654*, ed. C. Morton (2 vols., London, 1772), I, 203, Dec. 13, 1653; Folke Dahl, *Dutch Corantos 1618-1650 a Bibliography* . . . (The Hague, 1946); and by the same, "Amsterdam—earliest Newspaper Centre of Western Europe . . .," *Het Boek* (1938), XXV, 170 ff.

[32] C. Visser, *Verkeersindustrieën te Rotterdam in de tweede Helft der Acht-iende Eeuw* (Rotterdam, 1927); Z. W. Sneller, *Geschiedenis van den Steen-kolenhandel van Rotterdam* (Groningen, 1946), pp. 60 ff.

been described conformed more nearly to the first than to the second type; a few, textiles and textile-finishing for example, seem to have had characteristics of both.

Amsterdam's industry was not, in general, remarkable for the size of its workshops. We have glimpses of a few large plants in which there was some division of labor, as the famous printing establishment of the Blaeuws which was one of the largest buildings in the city. It had nine presses dedicated to the nine muses, six copper-plate presses for printing maps and engravings, and a type-foundry.[33] Of the sugar-refining industry Fokkens wrote in 1662:

In this city there are now many large sugar-bakeries, more than 50, where the sugar is boiled and refined; these are large buildings, there being sometimes sugar to the value of f. 200,000 in a single sugarbakery; here there are caldrons of great depth into which the sugar is put, and boiled in white water that has stood over chalk. After the sugar has been boiled the necessary time, it is put in jars which these workshops have by thousands. Indeed a sugar-baker may have solely in jars and molds to the value of 50 to 60,000 guilders, and from top to bottom the storerooms may be so full that there is but one passageway for a man to go through, and these houses are commonly five and six stories high. There are three potteries in this city and one outside where nothing else is made except jars and molds for these sugarbakers, and with this they are constantly occupied.[34]

The first manufacture of crystal and other glass of fine quality in Amsterdam was established in the late sixteenth century. In 1619 its proprietor claimed that it represented an investment of f. 50,000 and employed 80 workmen. A rival furnace employed 50 men.[35] The manufacture of silks, and of mixed textiles such as camlets and mohairs, demanded a good deal of capital for the raw materials. This was usually supplied by importers of these materials, or by wholesale traders in them, who acted as entrepreneurs, paying wages to craftsmen

[33] There is a fine description of this establishment by Von Zesen, p. 215. When it burned down in 1672, the loss was estimated at f. 355,000. (Elias, *De Vroedschap van Amsterdam*, I, 475.)

[34] M. Fokkens, p. 334 (Translation.) In 1660 fire destroyed one of the largest refineries in the city at an estimated loss of f. 300,000. (*Ibid.*, p. 73.) In 1664 the Pereiras sold their refinery with its equipment for f. 45,000. (Herbert I. Bloom, *The Economic Activities of the Jews of Amsterdam*, p. 39.)

[35] Van Dillen, *Bedrijfsleven*, II, xxvi; Von Zesen, p. 211; Fokkens, pp. 305-306.

engaged in the manufacture, and later taking over the finished product for sale or export. These industries, while less centralized in organization than those of which we have just spoken, represented a large investment and much technical specialization. In 1643 a maker of caffa silks had ten looms in his house and four elsewhere in the city; in 1646 another *caffatier* owned fifteen looms placed in various houses.[36] David Rutgers de Jonge stated in 1667 that he kept some 150 looms at work on bourats, camlets, and silks.[37] Late in the century calico printeries represented a substantial capital investment in plant, supplies, and equipment.[38] Breweries, bleacheries, distilleries, soaperies, foundries, and various industries requiring mills—gunpowder for example—while technically simple, called for tools and equipment not always within the financial capacity of a small master.[39]

Foreign visitors frequently expressed astonishment at the number and versatility of Amsterdam's mills. This precocious development of the industrial machine was perhaps stimulated by efforts to offset the high level of wages and the expense of importing raw materials. On the mechanical side it probably owed much to Dutch experiment with windmills for pumping water from polders, and for grinding corn. In 1665 Amsterdam had seventy-four sawmills at work. By 1678 there were eighty, and we hear of mills used in throwing silk, printing ribbons, fulling and calendaring cloth, dressing leather, extracting oil, making gunpower, and rolling copper plates.[40]

Shipping continued to command capital to unguessable—certainly large—amounts, but the rivalry of Zaandam where building could be done more cheaply, was keenly felt. In the

[36] Van Nierop, "De Zijdenijverheid van Amsterdam," *Tijdschrift* XLV, 165.
[37] *Brieven aan Johan de Witt,* eds. Fruin and Japikse, II, 384.
[38] W. J. Smit, *De Katoendrukkerij in Nederland tot 1813* (Amsterdam, 1928), pp. 70 ff., 124.
[39] Interesting glimpses of tools and equipment in use in various Amsterdam crafts are afforded by advertisements of businesses for sale, or those, seeking customers, culled by Dr. van Nierop from the *Amsterdamsche Courant,* 1667-1794: "Gegevens over de Nijverheid van Amsterdam . . .," *Jaarboek,* XXVII, 261 ff.
[40] G. J. Honig, "De Molens van Amsterdam," *ibid.,* XXVII, 79 ff.; Fokkens, pp. 334-335; Van Dillen, *Bedrijfsleven,* I-II, *passim;* S. Hart, "Een Bijdrage tot de Geschiedenis van de Houthandel," *De Zaende* (Feb. 10, 1948), III, 58, note.

economical construction of flutes the village had surpassed the
metropolis by the middle of the century, and though the Admiralty, East-India, and some private yards continued to build
for the navy and the ' dangerous ' trades, and to fill commissions for foreign powers, in this field too the competition of
lower building costs in Rotterdam as well as in Zaandam, was
inescapable.[41] In the late years of the century the competence
of the Admiralty of Amsterdam to keep abreast of advances
in naval construction in other countries would seem to have
declined.[42] It is significant that the English consul at Amsterdam in the nineties regarded the city as pre-eminently a timber
market and Zaandam as the place where the timber was built
into ships.[43]

Though not the greatest shipbuilding center, Amsterdam retained her standing as the port most frequented by shipping
wherever built or owned. In the second half of this century
and perhaps earlier, it had become the common practice of merchants to charter ships according to the needs of their trade,
or to pay freights for the carriage of their goods. Transport
was thus becoming a specialized economic function, distinct
from the trade carried. Amsterdam was well equipped to
furnish ships and shipping space, and many Amsterdammers
with capital to invest put it into ships to be hired out or
operated for freight.[44]

The vigorous initiative of industrial capitalism in Amsterdam in this period was cramped by the conservatism of municipal policy. By upholding the ban on industrial activities in
rural areas, Amsterdam was refusing to cheapen production

[41] S. Lootsma, *Historische Studiën over de Zaanstreek*, p. 179 ff.
[42] J. C. de Jonge, *Geschiedenis van het Nederlandschen Zeewezen*, III, 146
ff.; IV, 257 ff.
[43] *A Description of Holland . . . by an English Gentleman*, p. 17; Hart,
De Zaende, III, 58-59; Von Zesen, p. 172.
[44] Diferee, p. 346; Christensen, pp. 144 ff., 165 ff., 268. Of the 382 Dutch
ships measured and branded in the years 1647-1648 for the carriage of timber
from Norway, 58 per cent had been measured in Amsterdam, and were recorded
as " belonging " to that port, but most of the shipmasters came from ports of
Friesland and North Holland, and the vessels they captained had doubtless
been built in various maritime towns and villages of the Netherlands, though
they were chartered and freighted in Amsterdam which supplied the capital
and commodities required for the Norway trade. (Schreiner, " Die Niederländer und die Norwegische Holzausfuhr im 17. Jahrhundert," *Tijdschrift*,
XLIX, 305-306.)

costs by putting out manufacturing processes in the villages, or to sanction investment in village industries. The prohibition was not completely effective, but it was restrictive. Further, the city continued the gild system of industrial control, with methods of supervision and dictation congenial to that system. Amsterdam was, to be sure, less gild-ridden than more purely industrial cities. Most of the newer export industries—glass, sugar, gunpowder, tobacco-spinning, calico-printing, diamond cutting—and some of the older ones in which merchant capital had long been interested—soap-boiling, rope-making, brewing and malting, oil-pressing—had no gilds. But the number of gilds in the city increased in this century, and local exclusiveness which demanded protection against competition from other Dutch towns and from abroad, waxed stronger. The merchants of Amsterdam are generally found resisting such demands, but the tide was running strongly against them in the late decades of the century. Gilds were closely supervised by the municipal government, and emphasis in gild charters was shifting from protection of the craftsman in a local market, to control of employment and wages in the interest of employers competing in a world market. The city fathers found gild machinery useful too for the enforcement of elaborate technical prescriptions of which they were inordinately fond. Pieter de la Court summed up his condemnation of gild control of industry with the assertion: " That for the most part all Trades and Manufactures manag'd by Guilds in Holland, do sell all their Goods within this country to other Inhabitants. . . ." [45] Between the regulatory zeal of the *Vroedschap* with its machinery of enforcement and the rigidity of the gilds, freedom of industrial experimentation, enterprise and organization, and that flexibility of adjustment to the market which is the life of competitive industry, were grievously hampered.[46]

Of one phenomenon of industrial capitalism, labor unrest, only slight indications appear in the records of seventeenth-century Amsterdam. The clearest glimpse of it is found in the cloth-finishing industry in which a large number of wage-earners was employed, and a capitalist organization along

[45] *True Interest*, pp. 74-75.
[46] On the development and character of Amsterdam's gilds in this century: Van Dillen, *Bedrijfsleven*, I, x; II, x ff.; Brugmans, " Handel en Nijverheid," *Amsterdam*, II, 197 ff.

putting-out lines was of long standing. The so-called *droogs-cheerdersynoden,* an inter-city association of employer groups or gilds concerned with cloth-finishing, represented that industry in nine towns of Holland, Amsterdam being one. The aims of organization were to concert and maintain a common wage and employment policy, and to repress what seems to have been a widespread restlessness among clothworkers.[47] That there should have been relatively little demonstration of proletarian discontent is explicable rather by the absence or weakness of workingmen's organizations, than by an absence of grievances. The plight of Amsterdam's artisans was hard. The cost of living was high, and employers looking around for some way of reducing production costs were apt to hit upon wages as the most depressible item.

What has been said might give the impression that Amsterdam's industrial investment was confined to manufacturing activities carried on within her walls, but in this as in other comings and goings of capital and enterprise it is difficult to say where Amsterdam begins and ends. As early as the fifteenth century her citizens owned or held shares in the shipping of near-by villages, and in the next century Amsterdam capital was interested in ships whose home ports were towns on the Zuyder Zee, or in North-Holland or Friesland.[48] In the seventeenth century Amsterdam merchants and soap-boilers owned or shared ownership in Haarlem bleacheries.[49] We find Amsterdam interested in the manufacture of cloth in Delft and Kampen; in cloth-finishing workshops of Leiden; in a glass-furnace in Middelburg; a paper-mill in Gelders; a brewery and a foundry in Rotterdam.[50] In Zaan villages Amster-

---

[47] *Bescheiden betreffende de Provinciale Organisatie der Hollandsche Laken-bereiders,* ed. N. W. Posthumus [Werken uitgegeven door het Historisch Genootschap, 3rd ser., no. 38], Amsterdam, 1917. In 1621 there would seem to have been discontent among workmen in the hat-making industry— enough, at least, to suggest to employers the desirability of organization, though foreign competition was also alleged. Van Dillen, *Bedrijfsleven,* II, ix.

[48] Van Dillen, *Bedrijfsleven,* I, 191, 195, 220, 771; Van Ravesteyn, pp. 24 ff.; Christensen, pp. 39 ff. S. Lootsma, "De Zeevaart van Hindeloopen in de Zeventiende en Achttiende Eeuw," *Economisch-historisch Jaarboek* (1940), XXI, 241.

[49] S. C. Regtdorzee Greup Roldanus, *Geschiedenis der Haarlemmer Bleekerijen* [Economisch- en Sociaal-historische Onderzoekingen, no. 5, 's-Gravenhage, 1936], pp. 22, 105, 173, 207 ff.

[50] Van Dillen, *Bedrijfsleven,* II, 109-110, 466-467, 596-597, 612-614, 657,

dammers owned or held shares in bleacheries, train-cookeries, and mills.[51] Even without investment Amsterdam merchants or wholesalers could exert capitalistic pressure on the industries of other towns, as they did in the case of the biscuit manufacture of two Zaan villages, and seem to have done as principal customer of potteries in the vicinity of Leiden.[52] Of industrial investment in foreign countries something has already been said in regard to the munitions and metallurgical industries of Sweden, and we shall return to the subject later.[53]

755 ff.; *Bronnen tot de Geschiedenis van de Leidsche Textielnijverheid,* ed. N. W. Posthumus (Rijks Geschiedkundige Publicatiën, 6 vols., nos. 8, 14, 18, 22, 39, 49, 's-Gravenhage, 1910-1922), IV, xii; J. W. Enschedé, "Papier en Papierhandel in Noord-Nederland gedurende de zeventiende eeuw," *Tijdschrift voor Boek- en Bibliotheekwezen* (1909), VII, 103.

[51] Greup Roldanus, p. 22; Honig, *Jaarboek Amstelodamum,* XXVII, 111 ff.

[52] Aris van Braam, *Bloei en Verval van het Economisch-sociale Leven aan de Zaan in de 17de en 18de Eeuw* (Wormerveer, 1944), 127 ff. In the studies made by Miss van der Kloot Meyburg of a production cartel of some 35 to 39 potteries in the vicinity of Leiden, it is evident that one purpose of organization was to stabilize prices. Since in the years 1659-1664 joint sales were made to dealers in Amsterdam, and in 1662 200,000 pieces, in other years 100,000 were sold to one of these dealers, it seems certain that the pressure came from Amsterdam. (B. W. van der Kloot Meyburg, "Een Productiekartel in de Hollandsche Steenindustrie in de Zeventiende Eeuw," *Economisch-historisch Jaarboek* [1916], II, 208 ff.; by the same, "Eenige gegevens over de Hollandsche steenindustrie in de Zeventiende Eeuw," *ibid.,* [1925], XI, 79 ff.) In this last-mentioned article the author suggests that the potteries were being financed by entrepreneurs, which also points towards Amsterdam. (*Ibid.,* pp. 91 ff.)

[53] See pp. 36 ff., 118 ff.

CHAPTER IV

SPECULATIVE TRADING IN COMMODITIES AND COMPANY SHARES—PUBLIC LOANS

In the second half of the seventeenth century a tendency on the part of capital, discernible earlier, to prefer speculative trading in commodities and company shares, and investment in public loans and annuities, in moneylending and insurance, to the toil and hazards of foreign trade, became more marked. As early as the mid-sixteenth century there had been speculation in grain futures in Amsterdam.[1] In the early seventeenth century herring, spices, and whale-oil, as well as grain, were objects of speculative trading. Gerard Malynes was entirely familiar with conditional and optional contracts as practiced in the Low Countries and at Rouen and Calais, and had himself made money trading in salt and corn:

And this bargaining is most proper for such and the like commodities, the price whereof doth quickly rise and fall, and are also commodious when a mans money is not so ready to buy much, and to make a great employment with little money, which happeneth upon some sudden advice many times unexpected, whereupon men are very hot either to buy or sell: which is much used in Flanders in buying of Herring, before they are catched, by "stellegelt," as they call it, that is by a summe of money agreed upon to be paid, if the partie doeth repent himselfe of the bargaine. . . .[2]

During the latter half of the century the Amsterdam bourse was the scene of spirited trading in commodity values, which included transactions in options and in futures. In general, speculative attention was confined to commodities of which market supplies were unpredictable before the arrival of the fleets which imported them. " They invent new ways of Trade,"

[1] J. G. van Dillen, "Stukken betreffende den Termijnhandel in Graan in de laatste Jaren der Zeventiende Eeuw," *Economisch-historisch Jaarboek* (1918), IV, 37; and by the same, "Termijnhandel te Amsterdam in de 16de en 17de eeuw," *De Economist* (1927), LXXVI, 507.

[2] *Consuetudo, vel, Lex Mercatoria* (2d. ed., London, 1686), p. 144. " Flanders," as so often in English usage in this Century, may be taken to mean Holland, or Holland and Zeeland.

wrote John Cary in bewilderment, " great quantities of Brandy being disposed of every Year, which are never intended to be delivered, only the Buyer and Seller get or lose according to the Rates it bears at the time agreed on to make good the bargains; such a Commerce in England would be of little Advantage." [3] Ricard, whose experience in such trading went back to the late seventeenth or the early years of the eighteenth century, distinguished clearly the different types of transactions. Dealings in options he considered especially risky, " *Car il y a dans ce Commerce mille et mille tours de finesse, et même bien Souvent de friponnerie, et il est comme impossible de ne s'y pas ruiner, si on s'y engage fort avant.*" [4] In 1698 the States General denounced by *plakkaat* a practice evidently not uncommon: the sale of large quantities of grain by persons who had none, or at least not the quantities of which they affected to dispose. Sales at time and transactions in options were forbidden, but continued notwithstanding. [5]

The relation between such speculative trading in commodity values, and the commodity trade—the buying and selling of commodities as such—was undoubtedly more intimate than it is today, and merchants were principal actors in both. The market supplies of a number of important commodities were virtually monopolized by small groups of Amsterdam merchants or wholesale traders. Thus we hear of a ring of Amsterdammers who bought up whale products and forced up prices, of an attempted corner in Italian silks, one in sugar, another in perfume ingredients, another in saltpetre, another in copper. [6] In the cases of a number of commodities—gen-

---

[3] John Cary, *An Essay on the State of England in relation to its Trade* . . . (Bristol, 1695), p. 124.

[4] Jean-Pierre Ricard, *Le Négoce d'Amsterdam* . . . (2d ed., Rouen, 1723), p. 62.

[5] *Groot Placaet-boeck*, IV, 1371-1372.

[6] For mention of the speculators in whale products: M. F. J. Smith, *Tijd-affaires in Effecten aan de Amsterdamsche Beurs* ('s-Gravenhage, 1919), p. 87; the attempted monopoly of Italian silks: N. W. Posthumus, " Eene Kartelo-vereenkomst in de Zeventiende Eeuw in den Amsterdamschen Zijdehandel," *Economische-historisch Jaarboek* (1920), VI, 215; a profitable speculation in sugar in which Andries Bicker, of a distinguished Amsterdam family, hazarded about f. 100,000: A. E. Sayous, " Die grossen Händler und Kapitalisten in Amsterdam . . .," *Weltwirtschaftliches Archiv* (1938), XLVII, 126-127; for the ring of traders in perfume ingredients: " Gegevens betreffende de ' Oprechte Hollandsche civet,' " ed, I. Prins, *Economisch-historisch Jaarboek* (1936), XX,

erally such as came on the market in limited supply—we may infer from the stability of prices on the Amsterdam bourse over a period of years that trading in these commodities was practically confined to a group of dealers or importers acting in concert to maintain prices. In 1649 an agent of the English Commonwealth inquired of "a good discreet man" in Amsterdam whether saltpetre were cheap or plenty, and what price it bore.

> He told me, that for many commodityes, some few men had the cheife trade in them, and only such and such brokers knew the price of them. . . . That all the salt-peter of Poland, and that of the old store of the East-Indies, was all bought up into particular men's hands, expecting that through the warrs in Poland with the Cossacks it might grow dearer. That the price currant at the present of salt-peter refined was about 38 and 39 guylders the Amsterdam hundred. That there was a possibility of its fall a guylder or two, through the quantity lately brought from the East-Indyes, and through a great expectation and probability of a peace in Poland.[7]

This tendency towards combination implied in the price behavior of some 232 commodities for longer or shorter periods in the first half of the century, affected more than double that number in the second half, and was to be much extended in the eighteenth century.[8]

Purely financial speculation in company shares began in Amsterdam early in the seventeenth century, and was not practiced elsewhere on a like scale until the last decade when the London stock market rose like a rocket.[9] To induce the towns

3 ff.; for a working monopoly of saltpetre supplies in 1649: *A Collection of the State Papers of John Thurloe . . .*, ed. T. Birch (7 vols., London, 1742), I, 126; and for what would seem to have been an understanding among traders in copper: *Correspondance Administrative sous le Règne de Louis XIV*, ed. Depping, III, 409.

[7] *State Papers of John Thurloe*, I, 126.

[8] Posthumus, *Nederlandsche Prijsgeschiedenis*, I, lxxviii.

[9] On the history of trading in actions on the Amsterdam bourse, see Richard Ehrenberg, "Die Amsterdamer Aktienspekulation im 17. Jahrhundert," *Jahrbücher für Nationalökonomie und Statistik* (3rd ser., [1892]), III, 809 ff.; M. F. J. Smith *Tijd-affaires, passim*. In a defense of speculative trading in East-India actions, presumably drawn up by Isaac Le Maire and his associates in 1609 or 1610, it is asserted that such trading was not confined to Amsterdam and Middelburg, but was being practiced at Hamburg, Frankfort, Cologne, Rouen, and elsewhere. (Van Dillen, "Isaac Le Maire et le Commerce des Actions de la Compagnie des Indes Orientales," *Revue d'Histoire Moderne* [1935], X, 125.) If so, the trading in these cities must have been too small, too occasional, and too unorganized to attract attention and recording.

of the maritime provinces which had already embarked on trade to the East to merge rivalries and combine capitals in a powerful monopoly, the United East India Company had been organized on the lines of a cartel consisting of six local chambers, though the company traded as a unit and dividends were the same percentage of invested capital for all chambers. Market dealings, however, were practically confined to the shares (actions) of the Amsterdam chamber, " this because there is much more money in Amsterdam than in the other chambers, where trading is not so constant and one does not find at any moment, as at Amsterdam, buyers for whatsoever quantity." [10] Because of this negotiability and notwithstanding the equality of dividends, actions in the chamber of Amsterdam were usually quoted at considerably higher prices than actions in other chambers.[11]

The game sprang into public notice in 1609 with the efforts of an association of bears, headed by Isaac Le Maire, sometime of Antwerp, to depress the price of East India actions then selling at 300.[12] Announcement of a West India Company in 1621 was a signal for excited trading in the actions of that company even before subscription had opened.[13] Repeated efforts of the States General to put a stop to the sale of actions by persons who owned none, to buyers who were not always able to pay for them, failed as repeatedly. Only

[10] Translated from the " Mémoire touchant le négoce et la navigation des Hollandois . . .," ed. P. J. Blok, *Bijdragen en Mededeelingen* (1903), XXIV, 294. The trade was almost necessarily limited to actions in the local chamber because of the requirement that all transfers must be recorded in the office of the chamber and in the presence of the seller. (Van Dillen, " Isaac Le Maire," *Revue*, X, 19.) On the organization of Dutch commercial companies see, S. van Brakel, *De Hollandsche Handelscompagniën der Zeventiende Eeuw* . . . ('s-Gravenhage, 1908), especially the introduction, pp. xxix ff.

[11] Le Maire and his associates asserted that it was the very negotiability of actions in the Amsterdam chamber which caused them to sell at a premium of from 3 to 5 per cent over those in other chambers. (Van Dillen, " Isaac Le Maire," *Revue*, X, p. 125.) In 1694 Le Moine de l'Espine held the same opinion (*Le Négoce d'Amsterdam*, pp. 87 ff.) A pamphleteer of 1688 stated that Amsterdam actions were priced from 70 to 80 per cent higher than those of Delft and Enkhuysen, and sometimes 150 to 155 per cent higher than those of Zeeland (M. F. J. Smith, *Tijd-affaires*, pp. 70-71). See also the incomplete price quotations of Joseph Penso de la Vega for the same year (*Confusion de Confusiones* . . . [Amsterdam, 1688], p. 94).

[12] Van Dillen, " Isaac Le Maire," *Revue*, X, 5 ff., 121 ff.

[13] M. F. J. Smith, p. 56.

in 1689 was the policy of repression abandoned, when Amsterdam undertook to regulate and to tax the traffic in actions.[14] By this date speculative trading had reached a strikingly modern stage of expertness. A dramatic description of the technique had appeared in Amsterdam the previous year, appropriately entitled: *Confusion de Confusiones: Dialogos Curiosos entre un Philosopho Agudo, un Mercader Discreto y un Accionista Erudito, descriviendo el Negocio de las Acciones.* . . . The author, Joseph Penso de la Vega, was a veteran *accionista* who, by his own account, had made and lost five fortunes in this seductive form of gambling. He explained lucidly the various types of sale, the arts of time bargains, optional sales, buying on margin, " ducat-actions " by which small speculators followed the market, winning or losing a ducat for every point of rise or fall in the price of actions, and the *cabalas* of bulls and bears—the latter called *" misantropos de las acciones."* [15] Fixed liquidation days (*rescontre*) when a number of mutually contingent contracts were settled, had become customary.[16] There were brokers whose entire business was in actions.[17] In the second half of the century Portuguese and Spaniards, La Vega among them, seem to have been inveterate and numerous in playing the Amsterdam market in actions. " The Jews are the chief in that Trade, and are said to Negotiate 17 parts in 20 in the Company; These Actions are bought and sold four times a day, at 8 in the Morning in the Jewes-street, at a 11 on the Dam, and 12 and at one a Clock upon the Exchange, and at six in the Evening on the Dam, and in the Colleges or Clubs of the Jews until 12 midnight. . . ." [18] To minds less acute this trading was highly puzzling: " One sees . . . that without possessing

---

[14] *Groot Placaet-boeck,* 1, 553 ff., 665 ff.; III, 1307-1308; M. F. J. Smith, pp. 56 ff., 72 ff.

[15] This treatise of La Vega was well summarized by Ehrenberg in his article " Die Amsterdamer Aktienspekulation . . .," referred to in note 9, above. For descriptions of the trading methods mentioned above, see *Confusion,* pp. 47 ff., 226 ff.

[16] M. F. J. Smith, p. 6; Van Dillen, " Isaac Le Maire," *Revue,* X, p. 21.

[17] Ehrenberg, " Die Amsterdamer Aktienspekulation," *Jahrbücher,* III, 819, 824.

[18] *A Description of Holland . . . by an English Gentleman* (1701), p. 40. See also, Van Dillen, " De Economische Positie en Betekenis der Joden," *Geschiedenis der Joden in Nederland,* I, 585.

actions or even a desire to acquire any, one can carry on a
big business in them, and indeed there has never been, perhaps, a greater. . . . The seller, so to speak, sells nothing but
wind and the buyer receives only wind." [19]

It was on the Amsterdam bourse in this period that the
share completed its evolution from subscription of money to
any amount in a trading venture, recoverable only when the
enterprise or company should be terminated and the joint
stock wound up, to a unit of investment value in a permanent
undertaking which implied no active participation in the
business thus financed, and which the investor could sell or
dispose of at will.[20]

Of speculation in the *agio* of bank money over *courant*
there is less information, and still less about speculation in
the precious metals, in exchange, and in insurance, though
it is certain that these possibilities were not overlooked.[21]

Some wealthy and conservative Amsterdammers looked upon
their holdings of East-India actions as income-bearing investments, not as counters for speculation. From this point of
view actions of other chambers were no less desirable than
those of Amsterdam. Towards the end of the century 108 Amsterdammers were holding about three-eighths of the capital
stock of the Zeeland chamber, and Amsterdam capital was
similarly interested in other chambers. More than half of
the entire capital of the company was owned in Amsterdam.[22]

[19] "Mémoire touchant le négoce et la navigation des Hollandois . . .," ed.
P. J. Blok, *Bijdragen* XXIV, 291. (Translation) The real *windhandel* at its
hurricane stage was to occur synchronously with the same phenomenon in
London and Paris in the first quarter of the eighteenth century.

[20] S. van Brakel, pp. xxix ff.; Van Dillen, "Nieuwe Gegevens omtrent de
Amsterdamsche Compagniën van Verre," *Tijdschrift voor Geschiedenis* (1930),
XLV, 350 ff. On early difficulties in trading in actions of unequal values, and
the gradual standardization of the action at a par of f. 3,000: Van Dillen,
"Isaac Le Maire," *Revue*, X, 19-20. Even in the eighteenth century actions
differing widely in value from one another and from the norm were still
extant. (Smith, p. 39.)

[21] On speculation in the *agio*, Van Dillen, "The Bank of Amsterdam,"
History, pp. 90-91; Sneller, *Rotterdams Bedrijfsleven*, pp. 123, 136; Wagenaar,
Amsterdam, III, 539. Speculation in insurance is mentioned by G. W. Kernkamp, "Amsterdamsche Patriciërs," *Vragen des Tijds*, XXXII, 25, 31. Speculative dealings in the monetary metals have been briefly touched upon, above,
p. 53, and references to such practices occur frequently in Van Dillen, *Bronnen tot de Geschiedenis der Wisselbanken*, I, e.g., pp. 227 ff.

[22] H. Brugmans, *Opkomst en Bloei van Amsterdam*, p. 134. Louis Trip of

In the West India Company the city's stake was proportionately almost as great, though not so valuable. A paper undated but probably drawn up in 1667, estimated Amsterdam's investment in that company at more than half the total capital, and affirmed that the metropolis had advanced capital to other chambers.[23]

Instead of drawing in fresh capital by enlarging their original capital stocks, both companies preferred to borrow to meet current expenses. The debentures (*obligatiën*) of the East India Company were, like actions in that company, in demand as investments.[24] The West India Company, whose history in this century was checkered with vicissitude, at its reorganization in 1674 owed a large debt to its creditors and to those who had deposited funds with the company. The latter fared badly in the reorganization, recovering only 30 per cent of their deposits, but the former were repaid florin for florin, which may account for the fact that the company, despite renewed misfortunes, was still able to borrow at 4 per cent in 1694.[25]

For the prudent, whether of great or modest means, a relatively safe investment was available in loans to the city of Amsterdam, the province of Holland, or the United Provinces. The Dutch were the first of northern peoples to win public confidence for this method of anticipating revenue, and the credit of the metropolis, of a few other towns of the republic, of the richest province and—though to a lesser degree —of the federation, was a singular phenomenon in an age when most European governments were either chronically bankrupt like Spain and Austria, or tottering on the edge of that abyss like Stuart England or Bourbon France. " Holland

Amsterdam had more than half his East-India holdings in actions in the chambers of Enkhuysen and Hoorn. (Sayous, " Die grossen Händler und Kapitalisten," *Weltwirtschaftliches Archiv*, XLVII, 135.)

[23] Gemeente Oud-Archief, Amsterdam, Arch. Burgem., Handel 3, L W 7 N 2. " Eenige Consideratien nopende het seer importante benefitie ende het groot interest dat dese Staat Amsterdam heeft, in de herstellinge van de West Indische Compagnie boven d'andere steden ende leeden van de Provintien . . ."

[24] Kernkamp, " Amsterdamsche Patriciërs," *Vragen des Tijds*, XXXII, 25, 31. Of the f. 1,000,000 in debentures, paid off by the East India Company in 1670, f. 683,000 had been raised by the Amsterdam chamber. (Smith, p. 67.)

[25] Le Moine de l'Espine, *Le Négoce d'Amsterdam*, pp. 92 ff. See also a critical study of this work by Lucas Jansen, " *De Koophandel van Amsterdam* " *een Critische Studie van Jacques Le Moine de l'Espine* . . . (Amsterdam, 1946), p. 22.

being the Country of the World, the best skill'd in raising of
Money, from whence the Officers belonging to the Treasuries
of the most part of the Princes of Europe have extracted all
their Knowledge." [26] Sir William Temple observed with ad-
miration that the provincial debt of Holland, bearing interest
at 4 per cent, was carried

With so great ease and exactness both in Principal and Interest, that
no Man ever demands it twice; they might take up whatever Money
they desired. Whoever is admitted to bring in his Money, taking it
for a great deal of favour; and when they pay off any part of the
Principal, those, it belongs to, receive it with Tears, not knowing how
to dispose of it to Interest, with such Safety and Ease. And the common Revenue of particular Men lies much in the Cantores, either of
the Generality, or the several Provinces, which are the Registries of
these publique Debts. [27]

Until the terrible threat of the French invasion in 1672, the
debentures of Holland were exchangeable for cash at par,
" So," continued Temple, " whoever has a Bill of any publique
Debt, has so much ready Money in his Coffers, being paid
certainly at call, without charge, or trouble; and assign'd over
in payment, like the best Bill of Exchange." [28]

The elasticity of Dutch finance in time of war aroused an
exasperated respect in the republic's enemies who vainly antici-
pated the pleasure of seeing it break down. In the summer
of 1664, when war with England loomed, a loan of f. 1,000,000
at 3 per cent was subscribed in two days in Amsterdam. [29] Six
months later the English resident reported hopefully: " I do
assure you that every penny for this Sumers Equipage must be
taken up at interest which is now doing, and enough ods to
get it at foure per centum whereas those of Amsterdam said
they made no doubt but to helpe the States of Holland to as
much money as they pleased at three . . ." [30] But a few weeks
later: " As to the 3. millions which those of Holland do

[26] A New Description of Holland and the Rest of the United Provinces in
General (London, 1701), p. 12.
[27] Observaions upon the United Provinces of the Netherlands, ed. Clark,
p. 154.
[28] Ibid., p. 155.
[29] Calendar of State Papers . . . Venice, 1664-1666, ed. Allen B. Hinds (London, 1933), p. 30.
[30] Public Record Office, State Papers, foreign, Holland 174, ff. 40-41, To
Secretary Bennet, Jan. 4 (o.s.), 1664/5.

take up the respective summes were immediately subscribed by such as will lend the same, but especially that million at 8 per cent. for a life rent, and they are at this time mighty high." [31] Life rents were life annuities which bore a relatively high rate of interest because they were unredeemable and payments ceased at the death of the annuitant. In 1666, when England's war effort was already cramped for lack of funds, De Witt was said to have boasted "That of the last eight millions they had taken up, five yet remained untoucht and if they would take up twenty more at foure in the hundred hee was sure they might have it." [32] After peace had been signed at Breda, Englishmen returning by packet-boat from Holland reported "the great rhodomontade of the Dutch, who are paying off an old debt of 10 or 11 tons of gold [f. 1,000,000 to 1,100,000] which would willingly have continued in their banks, and this at the end of a great war to show the world how well stocked they are for a reversion." [33] In 1704 Bois-guilbert, lieutenant-general at Rouen, expressed despairing ad-miration of the credit enjoyed by the enemy cities of Amster-dam and Middelburg.[34]

The rates at which governments—municipal, provincial, or federal—could borrow, were fixed by resolution of their re-spective assemblies, but subscription had to be invited on terms likely to loosen the purse-strings of men as hard-headed and tight-fisted as the deputies and town-councillors themselves, who were in fact principal investors in these securities. In 1644 interest on the debt of Holland was reduced from 6½ to 5 per cent, and five years later interest on the federal debt was similarly reduced. In 1655, at the close of the first English war, another reduction, from 5 to 4 per cent, was voted. On the eve of the second English war the deputies of Amster-dam tried to induce the States of Holland to lower the rate to 3 per cent. "But there are so many of the Estates that

[31] Bodleian Library, Clarendon MS. 108, f. 200 v., To the Earl of Clarendon, Feb. 3/13, 1664/5.

[32] Public Record Office, State Papers, foreign, Flanders 34, f. 403. To Secre-tary Arlington, Brussels, July 23/Aug. 2, 1666.

[33] Calendar of State Papers, domestic series, 1667-1668, ed. M. A. E. Green (London, 1893), p. 30.

[34] Correspondance des Contrôleurs Généraux des Finances, ed. De Boislisle, II, 537.

have their monies upon the Cantores that this is no acceptable proposition to them."[35] It was not until the year 1672 that another conversion brought down the rate to 3¾ per cent. New loans could sometimes be floated by Holland at 3 per cent when the country was at peace; in war the rate might range from 4 to 6¼ per cent. In 1662 the provincial debt of Holland was about f. 120,000,000; in 1676 about f. 200,000,-000; in both years the interest was 4 per cent.[36] At the later date Charles II of England was paying not less than 10 per cent, and his brother of France in the neighborhood of 15 per cent. The credit of Amsterdam was maintained through a succession of wars. In January 1679, at the close of six years of war, the city's debt came to the moderate sum of f. 7,185,475, and the treasurer was urging the reduction of interest from 4 to 3½ per cent, pointing out that several towns of Holland— Alkmaar for instance—were paying only 3 per cent.[37]

At these relatively low rates lending to the local or federal government was a popular investment, and so widely were public debentures subscribed that the security of men of moderate means was inseparable from the security of state or city. Some of the wealthiest men of Amsterdam liked to have a backlog of public securities, as Louis Trip, who at his death in 1684 left f. 142,999 in debentures and short-term notes of the province of Holland; f. 9,000 in obligations of various Dutch towns; and f. 5,852 in redeemable annuities (*losrentebrieven*) also issued by municipalities.[38]

It must not be inferred from what has been said that Dutch

[35] Bodleian Library, Clarendon MS. 108, f. 99 v., Sir George Downing to Clarendon, Oct. 14/24, 1664. As the second English war drew to its close De Witt urged reduction of the rate to 3 per cent, but again failed to win legislative support. *Brieven, geschreven ende gewisselt, tusschen den Heer Johan de Witt . . . ende de Gevolmagtigden van den Staedt der Vereenighde Nederlanden* (6 vols., 's-Gravenhage, 1723-1725), III, p. 101.

[36] Lister, *Life and Administration of Edward, first Earl of Clarendon*, III, 217, Sir George Downing to Clarendon, Aug. 15/25, 1662; Public Record Office, State Papers, foreign, Holland 200, f. 313 v., Sir Gabriel Sylvius to Sir Joseph Williamson, March 7/17, 1675/6.

[37] H. S. M. van Wickevoort Crommelin, "Hoe Amsterdam aan Geld kwam," *De Economist* (1898), XLVII, 910-911. On Amsterdam finance, see also, H. J. Koenen, *Voorlezingen over de Geschiedenis der Finantiën van Amsterdam* (Amsterdam, 1855), pp. 19 ff.

[38] G. W. Kernkamp, "Amsterdamsche Patriciërs," *Vragen des Tijds*, XXXII, 30.

governments had arrived at the plenitude of fiscal wisdom, still less that the scheme of taxation by which public credit was upheld, had been framed with much consideration of ' ability to bear.' Government was in the hands of the *rentier* class, closely related through family and investment ties with the wealthy merchant oligarchies of the towns. Rich men, the saying went, " ran between the drops," while an array of excises on most consumer goods and on the commoner activities of living, bore with crushing weight on the peasant, the artisan, the seaman, and the fisherman. Amsterdam and other commercial towns of the federation resisted proposals to raise the customs or otherwise increase the burdens of trade and industry.

Although the investment value of public funds was recognized, they seem not to have been subject to market trading before the end of the third quarter of the century. As we have seen, the obligations of Holland were maintained at par, which discouraged speculation, and if there were fluctuations in the prices of other public securities, the fact that they were widely held in small lots made them less responsive to market manipulation than actions of the India companies, nor were they liable to sharp variations in price such as occurred in commodity values. The sudden downward plunge of these funds, those of Holland included, at the time of the French invasion, acted as an incentive to speculative trading, and thereafter prices were frequently quoted.[39] In 1673 the States General engaged to pay subsidies to the emperor in bonds at current prices on the bourse of Amsterdam. Trading in them soon quickened, and with time spread to other countries.[40]

---

[39] Information on price fluctuations of provincial debentures from May, 1672, when they were at par, to mid-April, 1673, when they stood at 80 per cent, is given by J. Grossmann, *Die Amsterdamer Börse vor Zweihundert Jahren* ('s-Gravenhage, 1876), pp. 111-112.

[40] *Ibid.*, pp. 56-57.

CHAPTER V

CAPITALISM IN COMMERCE

When all these uses of Amsterdam capital have been considered, the probability remains that the greatest employment of the city's capital resources in this century was in trade and activities consequent upon trade. The low interest paid by the principal public borrowers was an advantage to private business which could find credit without having to compete with necessitous governments in paying high interest charges.

It is a great Advantage for the Traffick of Holland, that Mony may be taken up by Merchants at 3½ per Cent. for a Year, without Pawn or Pledg; whereas in other countries there is much more given, and yet real Estates bound for the same: So that it appears, that the Hollanders may buy and lay out their ready Mony a whole Season before the Goods they purchase are in being, and manufactur'd, and sell them again on Trust (which cannot be done by any other trading Nation, considering their high Interest of Mony) and therefore is one of the greatest means whereby the Hollanders have gotten most of the Trade from other Nations.[1]

" In Holland," declared Josiah Child in 1668, " . . . any man that is a competent good Husband, Prudent and Careful in his business, may take up £500 or £1000 at 3 per cent. upon his own Note only, whereas in England where the present rate is double, the Usurers require three good Mens Bonds at the least for £500 at 6 per cent." [2] The Marquis de Pomponne, commenting on one of Colbert's projects to establish a reciprocal Franco-Swedish trade, noted that participants were to receive three-fourths for their wares in cash, and interest at 5 per cent on the remainder:

This procedure is common enough in Holland, where abundance of money makes it highly advantageous to obtain 5 per cent interest, when there is often difficulty in getting 4. I doubt whether this

---

[1] [La Court], *True Interest,* p. 33.
[2] *A Short Addition to the Observations concerning Trade and Interest of Money* (London, 1668), p. 10.

would be the case in our cities where, there being no organized companies, nor very rich merchants, few would content themselves with no more than this profit from the capital they have in trade.[3]

Of course interest rates were not the same for all borrowers: the risks involved and the relative easiness or tightness of money affected the rate in specific transactions. Loans on bottomry usually bore a higher rate than ordinary business loans, the risks being high. Thus the unfortunate West India Company, which had been paying 20 per cent on loans of this nature, was compelled to pay 30 per cent when news of English reprisals on the Guinea coast reached Amsterdam.[4] The ordinance of 1614 which fixed rates to be charged by the lending bank, required 16¼ per cent on pawns valued at less than 100 guilders, while for values of 500 guilders and up, the rate was 8 per cent, in 1656 reduced to 6 per cent.[5] In its early years the East India Company borrowed at 6¼ per cent, but this rate was progressively reduced until in the second half of the century the company was paying only 3½ per cent.[6] In 1633 we find Elias Trip contracting to pay the surprisingly high rate of 5 per cent on f. 90,000, perhaps because the security was a quantity of Swedish copper, for which there was then small demand.[7] There is, however, a fair consensus of contemporary statement that merchants in good standing could obtain credit at between 3 and 4½ per cent interest. Much of the willingness of Amsterdam capitalists to put their money out at interest in foreign countries may be ascribed to the fact that they could borrow in Amsterdam at these

---

[3] *Correspondance Administrative sous le règne de Louis XIV,* ed. Depping, III, 410. (Translation)

[4] Bodleian Library, Clarendon MS. 108, f. 75, Sir George Downing to Clarendon, Aug. 26/Sept. 5, 1664. Bottomry loans, for which ships or shares in ships were mortgaged, and which were repayable only on the safe arrival of the ships at their destinations, commonly represented emergency financing of a voyage.

[5] *Handvesten,* II, 679 ff.; Jansen, p. 20; H. J. Westerling, "Uit de Geschiedenis van de Bank van Leening in Nederland," *De Economist* (1914), LXIII, part ii, 699-700. In the second half of the seventeenth century this bank operated rather as a municipal pawnshop than as a bank making advances to merchants on the security of their commodity stocks or other assets. The financing of trade was carried on by private capital.

[6] Van Dillen, "The Bank of Amsterdam," *History,* p. 95.

[7] Gemeente Oud-Archief, Not. Arch. 667, f. 163. Notaris Jan Warnaarts, March 1, 1633.

low rates, and lend in England, France, or elsewhere at 6 per cent or better.[8]

The importance of low interest rates to Dutch trade was stressed by many English writers in this period. Because capital was easily found at low use, Dutch merchants were able to build and operate ships more economically than could their English competitors. They could make a profit from the fisheries, and from the bulky trades in grain, timber, metals, salt, and fish, in which cheap carriage was essential. They had an advantage too in branches of commerce which involved demurrage, long forbearance, and occasional loss, as in the Cadiz trade:

A great part of the Plate Trade from Cadiz is lost to the Dutch, who, by reason of the lowness of their Interest, can afford to let their Stocks lie beforehand at Civil and Cadiz, against the arrival of the Spanish Flota who sometimes are expected 3, 6, 9, and 12 Months before they come, . . . by which means they engross the greatest part of the Silver, whereas we, in regard our Stocks run at higher Interest cannot so well afford to keep them so long dead.[9]

Sir George Downing, hearing that a bill to raise the legal maximum rate of interest from 6 to 8 per cent was receiving consideration in the House of Commons, wrote testily to the Secretary of State:

It is very mischievous first to all trade and commerce, for this is a certaine maxime that all trade is govern'd by the rule of Interest of mony he that can borrow at Amsterdam for 3. or 4. per Cent. or if he have mony to let out can get but 3. or 4. per Cent. for it, this man if he get 6 per Cent. by his trade thinkes he does well, and he that must give 6 per Cent. will not trade unlesse he can get 8. or 9. per Cent. . . . and so if by reason mony is already at 6 per Cent. at London and but 4. at Amsterdam, those of Amsterdam do outtrade those of London, how

---

[8] See pp. 109, 122 ff.

[9] Josiah Child, *A New Discourse of Trade* . . . (2nd ed., London, 1694), preface, and pp. 51-52. There are many contemporary English comments on the low rate of interest prevailing in Holland, and the consequent advantage enjoyed by the Dutch, especially in shipbuilding and in the bulky trades, e.g., Sir Thomas Culpeper, "A Small Treatise against Usury," reprinted as appendix to the first edition of Child's *A New Discourse of Trade* (1668), p. 239; Roger Coke, *A Discourse of Trade* . . . (London, 1670), pp. 62-63; *Britannia Languens* (London, 1680), p. 318; Nicholas Barbon, "A Discourse of Trade" (1690) (*A Reprint of Economic Tracts*, ed. Jacob H. Hollander, 2d ser., no. 1, Baltimore, 1905), pp. 38 ff.; Charles Davenant, *Works*, ed. Whitworth, II, 294-295.

much more will they be able to out trade them when they shall pay but 4. at Amsterdam and 8. at London, so that in a word this is the way to make all turne Jews and Idle and to ruine the whole Commerce of the Nation.[10]

Dutch methods of purchasing and marketing filled their competitors with envy. They bought at seasons when prices were lowest, and stored the merchandise to await a sellers' market. Foreign visitors sightseeing in Amsterdam in this century seldom mentioned the city's warehouses in their descriptions, though these were as indispensable to Amsterdam's commerce as the ships in the harbor, and collectively may have represented a comparable investment of capital. A wealthy merchant, Arent ten Grootenhuys, who died in 1615, owned four warehouses in the city which were probably worth more than their assessed value of f. 15,000.[11] Louis Trip at his death in 1684 had property in the general storehouses of Uilenburg assessed at f. 9,910, and probably worth more.[12] From the descriptions of Fokkens and Von Zesen we have glimpses of the munitions storehouses near the Texel quay and, in the same neighborhood, the *kelders* in which brandies and tobacco were stored, which rented at from 1400 to 1600 guilders. On the Brouwersgracht were great storehouses four to five stories high, built with special precautions to strengthen them because there had been instances of the collapse of warehouses under too heavy burdens. Near the Haarlem locks were the herring-packeries; on the Warmussgasse the warehouses for books and precious goods of all kinds; on Osterburg the East India Company's storehouses. Products of the whale fishery were laid up in the ' Greenland ' storehouses.[13]

The storage of grain to meet both domestic and foreign demand had been an important factor in Amsterdam's rise, and that importance continued throughout the century. " Amsterdam," wrote Lewes Roberts in 1641, " is continually stored with 8, in 100,000 quarters, besides what is by trade

[10] Public Record Office, State Papers, foreign, Holland 174, f. 115, To Secretary Bennet, Feb. 14/24, 1664/5.

[11] Kernkamp, " Amsterdamsche Patriciërs," *Vragen des Tijds,* XXXII, 25.

[12] Sayous, " Le Rôle d'Amsterdam . . .," *Revue Historique,* CLXXXIII, pp. 272.

[13] M. Fokkens, pp. 63-64, 88; Von Zesen, pp. 172 ff.

daily sold away and vented." [14] In 1671 when landed interests in Zeeland were pressing the States General to raise the duty on imported grain, De Witt objected that such a measure would be of small benefit to Dutch agriculture since at that time there was stored in a few towns of Holland enough and more than enough grain to meet domestic needs for ten or twelve years.[15] The storage of spices to keep prices at a high level had begun early in the history of the East India Company, and was consistently pursued.[16] When in the course of the third war with England a proposal was made in the States General to ban all English manufactures from the Netherlands, " reply was made that this could not be done so suddenly, because at Amsterdam and elsewhere there was for the value of above ten millions of flanders monys of English manufacturies in the hands and in the houses of many merchants, and if such should be forbidden, it would be the ruin of so many thousand families." [17] On the eve of the War of Spanish Succession Amsterdam merchants, foreseeing that it was going to be difficult to obtain French and Spanish wares, filled their storehouses with them to such a point of congestion that ships coming in were unable to discharge their cargoes because there was no place in which to store them.[18]

Cheap buying meant reaching the producer, or ' buying out of the first hand ' as the expression ran. " When in any Foreign Country the Growth and Manufactures of that Place are very plentiful and cheap, such Commoditys are presently bought up by our Merchants, paid with ready Mony, and kept in their Magazins there, till the Season of Exportation and Shipping presents for other places. . . ." [19] On the French part

[14] *The Treasure of Traffike* (London, 1641), p. 89.

[15] F. N. Sickenga, *Bijdrage tot de Geschiedenis der Belastingen in Nederland,* p. 215.

[16] As early as 1609 a five years' supply of mace had accumulated. (Van Dillen, " Isaac Le Maire," *Revue,* X, 123. See also Temple's comment on the company's policy, *Observations,* ed. Clark, pp. 148-149.)

[17] Public Record Office, State Papers, foreign, Flanders 43, f. 199 v., James Nipho to Joseph Williamson, Dec. 8/18, 1673. On the importance of Amsterdam's business in the finishing and marketing of English woollen goods, see below, p. 94, n. 36.

[18] *Correspondance des Contrôleurs Généraux des Finances,* ed. De Boislisle, II, 121.

[19] [La Court], *True Interest,* p. 231.

of the island of St. Christopher in the West Indies in 1663, more than sixty Dutch warehouses, well stocked with goods, went up in flames, to an estimated loss of two million livres.[20] Samuel Lambe referred bitterly to the infiltration of Dutch factors into the export trade in English commodities:

Also, by their Banks they may be furnished in England by Exchange with ready money to buy the Native Commodities of the maker, at the first hand, and at the cheapest seasons of the year, as Lead, Tyn, Cloath, Bays, Sayes, Serges, Perpetuanaes, Stockings, &c having as is suspected, their English Packers at London, to buy such Goods there for their Accompts, and their Agents residing in the Countreys and Towns in England, where such Manufactures are made, and there buy them cheaper of the maker himself for ready money, by about 10 per cent. than the English Merchants can do at London. . . .[21]

By similar persuasions Dutch factors contracted with English fishermen for their catch before the season opened: " The use of the Hollanders and the Italians have been to disburse money beforehande, to the Fishermen, of the Weste Countrie and to take theire Pilchers at a Rate. . . ."[22]   And although Dutch fishermen could not engage in the cod fishery off Newfoundland since, having no shore rights, they could not dry their fish, Dutch fish-merchants crossed the ocean in the famine years of the early thirties to buy up English-caught cod and carry them off to Mediterranean markets.[23] Charges that French commodi-

[20] Stewart L. Mims, *Colbert's West India Policy* (Yale Historical Studies, no. 1, New Haven, 1912), p. 48.

[21] Samuel Lambe, *Seasonable Observations humbly offered to his Highness the Lord Protector* (London, 1658), pp. 9-10. In 1621 London brokers were complaining of the number and prevalence of Dutch brokers: " Of theis Dutch there are Twentie Brokers at least which doe daylie by their devices and multitude eate out the Freemen Brokers of this Cytie . . ." (*Commons Debate, 1621,* eds. Notestein, Relf, and Simpson, VI, 153, note.) For similar expressions of English resentment of Dutch infiltration into English trade, see Thomas Mun, *England's Treasure by Forraign Trade*, p. 81; also the remarks of Sir William Monson quoted below, p. 124.

[22] Public Record Office, State Papers 63/269, no. 80, " How to erect a Fishing upon the Coastes of England, Scotland, and Ireland " [1629?]. In a petition, undated but probably of the year 1633, the Master, Wardens, and Assistants of Trinity House complained that 16 to 18 foreign ships of two to three hundred tons each had called at western ports in that year to take on pilchards and Newfoundland cod for Spain or Italy; and that while the petition was being drawn there were eight Dutch ships taking on fish, and six already departed. *Calendar of State Papers, domestic series 1633-1634,* p. 367

[23] In the petition cited in the previous note it is asserted that 26 to 28 strangers' ships had gone to Newfoundland in that season to buy up fish

ties were being engrossed by Dutch merchants and factors were made by French ministers in 1656, and by Colbert in 1664.[24]

Although spontaneous exaggeration inheres in statements like these, it is clear that Dutch purchases were on a scale large for the time. It was part of their advantage over their rivals in the Norway trade that they took off timber by the shipload, paying custom according to the ship's tonnage, with consequent time-saving in the assessment of export tolls and money-saving by ingenious understatement of carrying capacity as vouched for in ships' papers.[25] They bought standing timber in Germany—entire forests, says Huet—to be felled on order.[26] Dutch ships trudged from island to island in Denmark to take off the entire grain surplus; and by cattle-ships and overland driving, some 20,000 to 30,000 head of lean beeves were brought from Jutland and Holstein to be fattened on the polders of Holland.[27] Dutch purchases of grain at Danzig

caught by English fishermen. (Ibid.) In the notarial register of Jan Warnaertsz. of Amsterdam a number of charter parties drawn up in April and May, 1633, are recorded by which ships were chartered to go to Plymouth or Falmouth to pick up a pilot, thence to Newfoundland, "en aldaer seijlen ende verseijlen van d'eene plaetse ende naer d'andere ende in te neemen visch tot een bekwaam lading toe," thence to Alicante, Marseille, Genoa, Livorno, or some other Mediterranean port to sell their fish. (Gemeente Oud-Archief, Not Arch. 668.)

[24] Brieven . . . Johan de Witt, I, 280; Letters, Instructions et Mémoires de Colbert, ed. P. Clément, II, annexes, p. cclxx.

[25] This was stipulated by the Dutch-Danish treaty of 1647. (Lieuwe van Aitzema, Historie of Verhael van Saken van Staet en Oorlogh [14 vols. in 15, 's-Gravenhage, 1657-1671] VI, 357 ff.) See also, Johan Schreiner," "Die Niederländer und die Norwegische Holzausfuhr im 17 Jahrhundert," Tijdschrift, XLIX, pp. 303 ff., 313.

[26] Mémoires sur le Commerce des Hollandois, p. 73. In the second half of the century more than five-sixths of the timber sold at auction in Zaandam, came from the Rhine and Elbe valleys of Germany. (C. A. Schillemans, "De Houtveilingen van Zaandam in de Jaren 1655-1811," Economisch-historisch Jaarboek [1947], XXIII, 241 ff., and especially the map on p. 252; also, "Een Bijdrage tot de Geschiedenis van de Houthandel" by S. Hart, De Zaende, III, pp. 53 ff., 65 ff., which modifies on some points the conclusions reached by Schillemans.) Schreiner's figures for the second quarter of the century point to the probability that the Amsterdam timber market depended in the main on Norwegian sources of supply. (See the article by Schreiner referred to in the preceding note, also the tables in his Nederland og Norge 1625-1650 Trelastutførset og Handelspolitik [Oslo, 1933], pp. 112 ff.)

[27] On the Danish grain trade: Axel Nielsen, Dänische Wirtschaftsgeschichte, p. 131; Molesworth, An Account of Denmark . . . , p. 28; J. C., Denmark vindicated . . . (London, 1694), p. 104; Sir Charles Whitworth, State of the

were a principal factor in determining prices there. In 1671 there was a failure of crops in Prussia and peasants were starving, but " Here have been larg parcells of Corne both Wheat and Rie: bought by the Hollanders for Italie: Soe that within these 6: weekes, they are advanced to almost doble the prices of what they were formerly: Rie being now sould at :150: wheat :260: gilders per last. . . ." [28] Dutch factors were said to buy French grains before the harvest, and wines before the vintage season.[29] Their purchases of wine in the Loire valley were said to have brought so much land under vines that not enough grain was produced in this fertile region to feed the population, and the Dutch market for brandy was held responsible for the shortage of wood caused by the *bruleries*.[30] Dutch factors were the best customers for both French and English West Indian sugars, carrying off the former in the face of Colbert's tariffs and prohibitions, and the latter from under the noses of the London sugar-bakers.[31]

Trade of Great Britain in its Imports and Exports . . . 1697 to 1773 . . . (London, 1776), p. xix. On the profitable business of fattening cattle from Holstein and Denmark: Nielsen, pp. 141, 166; *A Description of Holland: or the present state of the United Provinces* (1743), p. 351; Public Record Office, State Papers, foreign, Holland 174, f. 52, Sir George Downing to Secretary Bennet, Jan. 27, 1664/5; " Mémoire touchant le négoce et la navigation des Hollandois . . . ," ed. P. J. Blok, *Bijdragen en Mededeelingen* (1903), XXIV, p. 250.

[28] Public Record Office, State Papers, foreign, Poland 12 (no folio numbers), Francis Sanderson, Deputy Governor of the Eastland Company at Danzig, to Joseph Williamson, Sept. 16/26, 1671.

[29] [Jean Eon], *Le Commerce Honorable . . . composé par un habitant de Nantes* (Nantes, 1646), p. 89; Jules Mathorez, *Les Étrangers en France sous l'ancien régime . . . ,* II, 246.

[30] J. Mathorez, "Notes sur la Colonie hollandaise de Nantes," *Revue du Nord* (1913), IV, 10.

[31] For the rise of Amsterdam's sugar industry, see above, p. 62. On the pre-emption of French West Indian sugars by the refiners of Holland with collaboration from the Nantais, and the efforts of Colbert to prevent it: Mims, *Colbert's West India Policy,* pp. 44 ff., 260 ff.; Cole, *Colbert and a Century of French Mercantilism,* II, 50 ff.; P. M. Bondois, "Colbert et la Question des Sucres . . . ," *Revue d'Histoire Économique et Sociale* (1923), XI, 28 ff.; *Correspondance Administrative sous le règne de Louis XIV,* ed. Depping, I, 504-505. English customs records for 1698-1699 show that London exported only about 13,657 cwt. of sugar refined in England; the out-ports about 727 cwt. more. In this same year London exported about 125,211 cwt. of sugar in the state in which it had been imported; the outports an additional 14,294 cwt. Of these 139,505 cwt. of raw or partly refined sugar, Holland took about half, or 67,700 cwt., for her refineries. (Public Record

This discovers the true cause why the Sugar-Bakers of Holland can afford to give a greater price for Barbados Sugars in London, besides the second Freight and Charges upon them between England and Holland, and yet grow exceeding Rich upon their Trade: Whereas our Sugar-Bakers in London, that buy Sugars here at their own Doors, before such additional Freight and Charges come upon them, can scarce live upon their Callings, ours here paying for a good share of their Stocks six per cent, and few of them employ in their Sugar-works above six to ten Thousand Pounds at most: Whereas in Holland they employ twenty, thirty, to forty thousand Pounds Stock in a Sugar-House, paying but three per cent at most for what they take up at Interest, which is sometimes half, sometimes three quarters of their whole Stocks.[32]

Dutch traders were the best customers for West Indian and Maryland tobaccos,[33] and for Venezuelan cocoas which they continued to monopolize in the eighteenth century in spite of the privileges of the Caracas Company.[34] Holland was the chief continental market for English tin, and for English and Scottish coals.[35] For Swedish copper, Spanish wools, Bordeaux

Office, Customs 2/6.) In addition to the sugar re-exported from England, Dutch traders obtained large amounts of muscovado sugar smuggled out of the English West Indian islands to the Dutch island of St. Eustatius in order to evade the 4½ per cent duty levied in England. Dalby Thomas, "An Historical Account of the Rise and Growth of the West Indian Colonies . . . ," *Harleian Miscellany,* IX, 438.

[32] Child, *A New Discourse of Trade* (2d ed., 1694), pp. 22-23.

[33] On Amsterdam as a processing center for American tobacco, see above, p. 63. On the dependence of French tobacco-planters in the West Indies on the Dutch market in 1662: Mims, pp. 54-55; and for the dependence of the farmers of the tobacco monopoly in France, and of French consumers generally, on tobacco imported from Holland: Vertrees J. Wyckoff, *Tobacco Regulation in Colonial Maryland* (Johns Hopkins University Studies, extra vols., new ser., no. 22, Baltimore, 1936), p. 116; *Correspondance des Contrôleurs Généraux des Finances,* ed. A. M. de Boislisle and P. de Bretonne, II, 497; III, 357, note. On the Holland market for Maryland tobacco: Wyckoff, pp. 45, 53, 54, 76. In 1690 Dalby Thomas estimated that two-thirds of the colonial tobacco imported into England was re-exported to foreign markets. (" An Historical Account . . . ," *Harleian Miscellany* IX, 425.) The report of the Inspector General of Customs for 1698-1699 shows that Holland was then taking 8,900,000 lbs. of the 22,414,000 lbs. re-exported from England. (Public Record Office, Customs 2/6.)

[34] Roland Dennis Hussey, *The Caracas Company, 1728-1784* . . . (Harvard Historical Studies, no. 37, Cambridge, 1934), *passim.*

[35] George Randall Lewis, *The Stannaries a Study of the English Tin Miner* (Harvard Economic Studies, no. 3, Cambridge, *c.* 1907) pp. 59, 154; John U. Nef, *The Rise of the English Coal Industry* (London School of Economics and Political Science, Studies in Economic and Social History, no. 6, 2 vols., London, 1932), I, 84 ff., 92. Evidence of the increasing use of English and Scottish coals for industrial purposes in Holland is found in Van Dillen,

wines, Portuguese salt, and English draperies, Holland, and principally Amsterdam, was the continental market.[36] In 1640 an Amsterdam house bought up such quantities of Russian furs, forestalling the yearly mart at Archangel, that when the fair opened few were to be had.[37]

Dutch merchants and factors were accustomed to pay for their purchases partly in cash, and partly in bills of exchange on Amsterdam where their customers were usually glad to have funds. In selling they were willing to allow one or two years' credit. This procedure, which their foreign competitors were for the most part unable to emulate, gave the Dutch a broad margin of advantage, especially in the northern trades.[38]

Bedrijfsleven, II, 547-548; and in Z. W. Sneller, *Geschiedenis van den Steen-kolenhandel van Rotterdam*, pp. 70-71, 93.

[36] On the struggle by Amsterdam capitalists, notably Louis de Geer and Elias Trip, to monopolize Swedish copper exports: Van Dillen, " Amsterdamsche Notarieele Acten betreffende den Koperhandel," *Bijdragen en Mededeelingen*, LVIII, 211 ff.; E. W. Dahlgren, *Louis de Geer, 1587-1652*, I, 180 ff.; F. Breedvelt-Van Veen, *Louis de Geer, 1587-1652*, pp. 48 ff., 95 ff.

As to the practical monopoly (four-fifths of the export supply) of Spanish wool by the Amsterdam market: H. Brugmans, " Handel en Nijverheid," *Amsterdam*, II, 201; Diferee, *De Geschiedenis van den Nederlandschen Handel*, p. 207; and an anonymous tract, *A Brief Narration of the Present Estate of the Bilbao Trade* (London, 1650) p. 2.

In 1667-1668 23,360 tun of French wines paid import duty in Amsterdam. (H. Brugmans, " Statistiek van den In- en Uitvoer van Amsterdam," *Bijdragen en Mededeelingen, XIX*, 125 ff.) On the wine trade in general see Van Dillen, *Bedrijfsleven*, II, xxiv. In 1651, 104 out of 441 ships clearing from Bordeaux were Amsterdam ships. Their tonnage came to 19,904 t. out of a total of 62,822 t. Of the remaining 337 sail, 319 were Dutch, many of them undoubtedly bound for Amsterdam. (Théophile Malvezin, *Histoire du Commerce de Bordeaux depuis les origines jusqu'à nos Jours* [4 vols., Bordeaux, 1892], II, 272.)

On Dutch pre-eminence in the export trade of Setubal, Portugal's famous salt port: Diferee, p. 393; also, below p. 105.

Throughout this century Holland carried on a large business in finishing and marketing English draperies—a business in which Amsterdam had a considerable stake. (Astrid Friis, *Alderman Cockayne's Project and the Cloth Trade . . . 1603-1625* [London, 1927], *passim;* Van Dillen, *Bedrijfsleven*, II, xx.) Because of this interest efforts of Dutch cloth-manufacturers to exclude or to lay high protective duties on English woollen goods met with determined resistance in Amsterdam. (See the documents on this subject in Portefeuille Handel 10, Gemeente Oud-Archief, Amsterdam.) At the close of the century the United Provinces ranked second only to Spain as customer for these manufactures. (Computed from the Inspector-general's report on exports of English manufactures from Christmas 1698 to Christmas 1699, Public Record Office, Customs 2/6.)

[37] Scheltema, I, 172.

[38] On this effective combination of cash and credit: [La Court], *True Interest,*

Large purchases, liberal credit, and cheap transportation combined to keep Amsterdam prices on a level with those prevailing in places of origin.[39] In 1606 a member of the House of Commons maintained that the Dutch could sell English cloth dressed in the Netherlands and re-exported thence, more cheaply than the English trading companies could do.[40] A similar statement was made in 1622 by Gerard Malynes.[41] " I can confidently affirm," declared Samuel Hayne in 1685, " that Cargoes from Amsterdam or Rotterdam are made at least 10 per cent. cheaper than those in London can be, and consequently may be sold so in the Plantations. . . ." [42] The drawback was helpful to Hollanders in enabling them to sell English colonial sugars refined in Holland at a lower price than English refined sugars could be afforded.[43] They could undersell the English in tobacco, and in 1706 were supplying tobacco to the English navy.[44] Dutch factors were said to buy English coals at lower prices than English buyers must pay.[45] Martinus Tancken, resident of the king of Denmark at the Hague, observed in 1645 that Netherlanders could export Baltic products more cheaply than could the Eastlanders them-

p. 230; Savary, *Le Parfait négociant* bk. ii, p. 108; Ewald Bosse, *Norwegens Volkswirtschaft vom Ausgang der Hansaperiode bis zur Gegenwart* . . . (2 vols., Jena, 1916), I, 31; Boissonnade and Charliat, p. 49. In 1620 the English Eastland Company, and in 1650 the Levant Company, lamented the advantage enjoyed by the Dutch in their respective spheres of trade because these rivals paid in ready money. *(Calendar of State Papers, domestic ser., 1619-1623,* ed. M. A. E. Green [London, 1858], pp. 157, 211; *ibid., 1649-1650* [London, 1875], p. 12.) Samuel Lambe asserted in 1658 that ready money enabled Dutch factors to buy up English commodities more cheaply than could English merchants. *(Seasonable Observations, pp. 9-10.)*

[39] Bishop Huet ascribed to the Dutch " le secret de pouvoir donner des Marchandises à meilleur marché que les autres, & même de les faire trouver en Hollande, presque pour le même prix que sur les lieux d'où ils les tirent." *(Mémoires sur le Commerce des Hollandois,* p. 72.) On this point see also " Considerations on the East-India Trade . . ." 1701, reprinted in *A Select Collection of Early English Tracts on Commerce,* ed. J. R. McCulloch (London, 1856), p. 602.

[40] Friis, p. 238.

[41] *Lex Mercatoria* (1686), p. 65.

[42] *An Abstract of all the Statutes made concerning Aliens trading in England,* p. 11.

[43] Dalby Thomas, " An Historical Account . . . ," *Harleian Miscellany,* IX, 419.

[44] Wyckoff, p. 117.

[45] Nef, II, 411.

selves,[46] and a half-century later Bishop Huet stated that pitch and tar could be had as cheap in Holland as in Sweden.[47] At about the same time John Cary maintained that the Dutch were able to freight salt from Setubal, and timber, hemp, corn, pitch, etc., from the Baltic " at such rates that many times they are fetch'd thence by other Nations cheaper than they could do it from the Places of their Growth." [48] French wines and brandies, according to Savary, were carried to Norway at prices which French merchants could not equal.[49] As for French wines in Holland, " they have such store . . . that they sell it much cheaper than at Paris." [50] One must take such statements as indications rather than as substantiated facts.

It is not surprising that this strong position was occasionally used to exclude rivals and to fix prices. In Nantes in 1645 resident Dutch merchants and factors were well organized and high-handed. According to a complaint from their French competitors they had formed an association whose authority was as binding as law or religion, and whose intention was to monopolize the entire trade of the port to the discomfiture of the Nantais.[51] This charge was echoed by other writers, and made explicit in 1675 by Jacques Savary:

The Dutch commission merchants established at Nantes often form combinations *(sociétez anonimes)* for the purchase of wines and brandies, pricing them as they please; because the merchants cannot avoid passing through their hands. They act like upholsterers who, having offered a price for something, if it is not accepted on the spot, along comes another to bid, and offers less than the first. This procedure disconcerts the merchants so that they do not know what decision to make about the sale of their goods.[52]

---

[46] Diferee, p. 179.

[47] *Mémoires sur le Commerce des Hollandois* . . . , p. 59.

[48] *An Essay on the State of England in Relation to its Trade* (1695), pp. 123-124.

[49] *Le Parfait négociant*, book ii, p. 90.

[50] *A New Description of Holland, and the Rest of the United Provinces* (1701), p. 31.

[51] J. Mathorez, "Notes sur la Colonie hollandaise de Nantes," *Revue du Nord*, IV, 1 ff.; Henri Sée, " Un Document sur le commerce des Hollandais à Nantes en 1645," *Economisch-historisch Jaarboek* (1926), XII, 127 ff.; [Jean Eon], *Le Commerce Honorable, passim.*

[52] *Le Parfait négociant*, book i, pp. 375-376. (Translation.) For later testimony on the hold of Dutch merchants on the commerce of Nantes, see the memoire of Des Casaux du Hallay, deputy from Nantes to the Council of

Such tactics may have had some part in precipitating anti-Dutch disturbances in several French towns during the minority of Louis XIV, though there were political strains as well.[53]

Sometimes Dutch traders resorted to dumping goods on the market in order to embarrass their competitors. This was the unhappy experience of Prussian merchants from Kolberg and Königsberg who attempted to market their own grain in Amsterdam;[54] of the Cie. du Nord, trying to supply La Rochelle with timber in competition with the Dutch;[55] of a Yarmouth ship laden with red herring whose market at Marseille was spoiled by Dutch fish-merchants.[56] The Dutch East India Company was accused of forestalling and dumping by competing companies.[57] It was not often, however, that Dutch merchants had need of such weapons. Because they were the greatest buyers and the most obliging creditors they were almost indispensable, and merchants and dealers in other countries depended largely upon them. Denmark was a country without capital, and even in the sixteenth century Copenhagen merchants were said to be no more than factors of their Dutch employers.[58] During the seventeenth century this dependence increased. In 1673 Thomas Henshaw wrote from Copenhagen:

The news of the taking of Maestricht . . . gained no acclamation in this towne, which receives mony conveniencys from Holland, not only by the Kings tolls from those numerous Holland ships that trade continually in the Balticke seas, and the great quantitys of corne they take off these Islands, but almost all merchants and retailers here subsist by theyre Credit with Holland as our country Chapmen in England do by being trusted by London dealers, and in like manner these have time to pay theyr Principalls till in Reason they might have sould the commoditys. . . .[59]

Commerce, March 4, 1701, *Correspondance des Contrôleurs Généraux des Finances,* ed. De Boislisle, II, 491.

[53] Mathorez, *Les Étrangers en France,* II, 256-257; *State Papers of John Thurloe,* II, 541, 548; see also, the general denunciations by French ministers of Dutch trading methods in France, in the documents referred to in note 24, p. 91, above.

[54] E. Baasch, *Holländische Wirtschaftsgeschichte,* pp. 308-309.

[55] *Letters, Instructions et Mémoires de Colbert,* ed. Clément, II, 488.

[56] *The Naval Tracts of Sir William Monson,* ed. M. Oppenheim (Navy Records Society, 5 vols., London, 1902-1914), V, 312.

[57] *State Papers of John Thurloe,* II, 541.

[58] Nielsen, pp. 111-112.

[59] Public Record Office, State Papers, foreign, Denmark 19, f. 276, To Lord Arlington, July 1 (o.s.), 1673.

Near the close of the century Molesworth referred to Danish traders as "men of no Substance but indebted over head and ears to their Creditors at Amsterdam and Hamburg." [60] When the French Cie. du Nord offered to supply the Danish kingdom with French salt and to contract for the entire output of Norwegian copper mines, the Dutch resident observed mildly that it was doubtful whether trade could be diverted thus from a monied country to one where money was not to be had.[61] He was not surprised to learn that the vintners of Stockholm were resisting pressure from the Swedish king to import wines exclusively from places of growth, "because the Swedish wine-dealers have more credit in the Netherlands than in France, Spain, and Germany." [62] In 1675 when war between the States General and Sweden seemed imminent, the Swedish king suddenly ordered the seizure of all Dutch effects in Sweden. "Now," wrote the English envoy at Stockholm, "as this severe proceeding will tend to the great loss of the Hollanders, so it will ruine most of the Swedes Merchants whose books are found full of debts which they ow in Holland, which being now all forfited to the Crown, these Swedes who lived and traded upon the Credit given them by the Hollander, will now have no more. . . ." [63] Two years later tension had not abated, and the representative of the States General at Stockholm reminded the court "that not merely most of the furnaces but also most of the shops in this kingdom operate and are sustained by Dutch money and credit." [64]

Dutch mastery of French foreign trade in this century was asserted with varying degrees of resentment by Montchrétien

---

[60] *An Account of Denmark,* p. 119.

[61] "*Of de trafique uyt een pecunieus lant soude cunnen getransporteert worden naer plaatsen daer sulcx niet te vinden is, can qualijck gelooft worden.*" (Rijks Archief, Staten Generaal, Secrete Brieven, Denemarken 7272, From Le Maire, Copenhagen, Oct. 4, 1664.)

[62] *Ibid.* From the same, Jan. 8, 1664. (Translation)

[63] Public Record Office, State Papers, foreign, Sweden 9, f. 143, Sir Edward Wood, Stockholm, to Sir Joseph Williamson, June 30 (o.s.), 1675.

[64] "Wat voordeel de hollanders in dit rijck gebracht hebben, en dat niet alleen de meeste haemers maer oock de meeste winckels in dit Rijck op der Hollanders haer gelt en credit roulleeren en onderhouden worden." Rijks Archief, Staten Generaal, Secrete Brieven, Zweden 7283, From C. C. Rumpf, Sept. 4, 1677.)

(1615); by Jean Eon (1646); by French ministers in 1656; by Colbert throughout his more than twenty years in the royal service; and by Jacques Savary (1675). In the sixties and seventies Colbert and his royal master did their best to get this trade out of Dutch hands and into French through tariffs, discriminations, commercial monopolies, and war. All this was not without effect, and Dutch merchants began leaving the country long before the revocation of the Edict of Nantes. That event, which administered so severe a shock to Huguenot industry and commerce, hastened the exodus of foreign Protestants. But the treaties which closed the Franco-Dutch wars conceded favorable treatment to Netherlands trade, especially in the export of salt. Complete recovery was hampered by bigotry, mercantilism, and insecurity. A merchant writing in 1699 observed that the Dutch belittled the importance of the French trade because it was not what it had been, whereas it was still one of the most important branches of their commerce.[65] Arnould's figures for France's foreign trade in 1716 indicate that the United Provinces were taking 29.2 per cent of France's exports, and purveying 16.9 per cent of her imports.[66] Almost every step taken by Louis XIV's ministers to break the long commercial intercourse between the two peoples, evoked cries of protest from Frenchmen, especially from the wine merchants of Bordeaux and the exporters of crude sugars of Nantes, but also from a wide variety of interests ranging from makers of petty haberdashery, to landowners.[67] The invasion of the Netherlands in 1672 precipitated an epidemic of bankruptcies in the country which was winning all the victories.[68]

---

[65] " Mémoire touchant le négoce et la navigation des Hollandois," ed. Blok, *Bijdragen*, XXIV, 262. See also, H. Sée, " L'Activeté commerciale de la Hollande à la fin du XVIIᵉ siècle," *Revue d'Histoire Économique et Sociale* (1926), XIV, 26; and the extracts from the *mémoires* presented to the Council of Commerce in 1701 by the sieur Des Casaux, deputy from Nantes. Martin, *La Grande Industrie*, pp. 382-383.

[66] A.-M. Arnould, *De la Balance du Commerce . . . de la France* (3 vols., Paris, 1791), III, Chart I, A-B.

[67] For evidence on this point: *Brieven . . . Johan de Witt*. I, 340, 347, 399, 406, 457; II, 26, 91; *State Papers of John Thurloe*, V, 498; VI, 227; *Correspondance des Contrôleurs Généraux des Finances,* ed. De Boislisle, I, 40, 97, 106, 168, 184; *Correspondance Administrative sous le Règne de Louis XIV,* ed. Depping, III, 415.

[68] " . . . We heare that many Bankiers are turned Bankrout, — 4 att Lyons,

It was not only to the great merchants and wholesalers that the Dutch extended credit. They were assiduous in cultivating the goodwill and the business of the small trader, the fish-dealer, the vine-grower, the poor planter, even the shopkeeper. Lewes Roberts noted that Hollanders were as willing to do business on a small as on a large scale.[69] Trinity House complained that Dutch shipmasters made a practice of advancing money to English buyers of Norway timber, as an inducement to freight Dutch vessels.[70] Sir William Monson declared that the Hollanders were practically masters of the export trade in red herring from Yarmouth.[71] Said a member of Parliament in 1670: " The Tuckers and Weavers of Exeter to be made Factors in Holland, do the business for Holland Merchants." [72] We hear of a year's credit accorded planters in the English West Indian islands by Dutch traders, and Du Tertre stressed the friendly relations existing between these traders and French planters on St. Christophe in the fifties and sixties.[73] In 1701 the relations between Dutch merchants and French retailers in Paris and other towns were, in one Frenchman's opinion, entirely too cordial.[74]

Though so generally *non gratae* to kings, to mercantilists, and to competitors, the Dutch were not unwelcome in the communities to which they traded. During the Anglo-Dutch wars sympathy for the Netherlanders was widespread in Europe. " The Bourgeois is generally no frend to us," wrote

6 att Bourdeaux and 2 or 3 in this place." (Public Record Office, State Papers, foreign, France 135, f. 25, Thomas Chudleigh, Paris, to Joseph Williamson, Sept. 18/28, 1672.) " Je ne doute point que les banqueroutes qui arrivent journellement à Bordeaux n'altèrent extrêmement le commerce mais il est difficile d'y apporter du remède." *(Lettres, instructions et mémoires de Colbert,* ed. Clément, II, 662, Colbert to De Sève, Intendant at Bordeaux, Sept. 16, 1672.)

[69] Lewes Roberts, *The Merchants Mappe of Commerce* (1638), p. 120.

[70] British Museum, Lansdowne MS. 142 (Caesar Papers), f. 294.

[71] *The Naval Tracts of Sir William Monson,* ed. M. Oppenheim, V, 234-235.

[72] Anchitell Grey, *Debates of the House of Commons from the Year 1667 to the Year 1694* (10 vols., London, 1763-1769), I, 361.

[73] Sir Robert H. Schomburgk, *The History of Barbados* (London, 1848), p. 268; *Calendar of State Papers, colonial series, America and West Indies, 1669-1674,* ed. W. Noel Sainsbury, p. 290, Sir Charles Wheler, Governor of the Leeward Islands to the Council for Foreign Plantations, Dec. 9, 1671; Mims, pp. 46 ff.

[74] *Correspondance des Contrôleurs Généraux des Finances,* II, 490 ff.

the English ambassador from Paris in 1665, "their having so much dealing with the Hollander doth wholy backbyas them that way." [75] "All the [English] Merchants upon the coast [of Spain] complain of the Spanish partiality towards the Dutch." [76] Sir Gilbert Talbot, laboring to detach Denmark from the Dutch alliance, found Copenhagen filled with malicious rumors reflecting upon England, "purposely spread to feed the humours of this Comonalty, which by reason of theyre constant trade with the Hollanders is wholly carried in theyre affections toward them: nor is it the Comonalty alone, but many of theyre cheife men who stand that way affected." [77] In 1672, though the Swedish crown was allied with France, "The people of this country are generally well wishers to the Hollanders, and the greatest lye imaginable, if told in their favour, is presently believ'd." [78]

In Leghorn first reports of a Dutch victory in the four days' naval battle off the North Foreland in the summer of 1666 were received with enthusiasm: "The very Porters themselves in Troops of fifty run up and down the streets crying let the Dutch live. . . ." [79] There were pro-Dutch demonstrations in Martinique in 1665, and in Santo Domingo in 1671. [80] In Scotland sympathies veered towards the Dutch despite the state of war. [81] Even in certain of the English east-coast towns whose peacetime trade with Holland was large, solicitude for the enemy was expressed. Thus in 1672 the Secretary of State was informed from Yarmouth: "Wee are so dutchefied here, that a dutchman cannot be more deiected then generally our people are here for the sad condition wee

[75] Public Record Office, State Papers, foreign, France 120, f. 221 v., To Lord Arlington, June 17/27, 1665.

[76] *The Right Honourable the Earl of Arlington's Letters* . . . (2 vols., London, 1701), II, 82.

[77] Public Record Office, State Papers, foreign, Denmark 18, f. 9, To Lord Arlington, Jan. 20 (o.s.), 1666. See also the excerpt from a letter of Thomas Henshaw, above, p. 97.

[78] Public Record Office, State Papers, foreign, Sweden 8, f. 128, William Allestree, Stockholm, to Joseph Williamson, Oct. 29, 1672.

[79] *Ibid.*, State Papers, foreign, Tuscany 7, Memorial from Sir John Finch to the Grand Duke of Tuscany, June 27/July 7, 1666. (Copy.)

[80] Mims, pp. 101, 202 ff.; Cole, II, 9, 31.

[81] James Mackinnon, *A History of Modern Liberty* (4 vols., London, 1906-1941), IV, 293; G. D. Henderson, *Religious Life in Seventeenth-century Scotland*, p. 71.

understand the Hollanders to be in which I attribute to the Constant trade wee have with them in time of peace which they now want. . . ." [82] The compilers of the *Dictionnaire Universel de Commerce,* who were not always well disposed towards the Dutch for mercantilist reasons, nonetheless acknowledged handsomely as one factor in their commercial success, " *cette franchise, et cette bonnefoy dont ils en usent avec tous leurs Correspondans, de quelque Nation qu'ils soient.*" [83]

Throughout the seventeenth century Dutch predominance in European trade was under attack from all commercially ambitious states. Rulers of the Scandinavian kingdoms resorted to the usual mercantilist measures to stop what they considered exploitation of their countries' trade and resources, and listened with interest to English and French designs to oust the Hollanders from the Norway and Baltic trades. The court of Sweden was particularly hostile to the republic, but even when the two powers were at war in 1659, Edward Mountagu, who commanded the English squadron in the Sound, was given to understand that the Swedish king would never agree to an alliance with England which should exclude the Dutch from the Baltic, " which he cannot doe, unlesse the trade of Dantzick and the whole Baltique were assured to be taken off his hands by the English. . . ." [84] In 1665 when the English government was again angling for an Anglo-Swedish alliance against the States-General, the Swedish chancellor inquired anxiously how far England was prepared to go in demands on the Dutch, " because though Sweade judged it very convenient and just that Holland should be thoroughly humbled, and made make amends for Injurys and Insolencys committed; yett that it was not the Interest of the King of England or Sweade, that Holland should be totally undone." [85] And again in 1673 when the fortunes of the republic were low, the king of Sweden sent Count Tott to the French camp with instruc-

---

[82] Public Record Office, State Papers, domestic, 29/312, Richard Bower to Joseph Williamson, June 24, 1672.

[83] *Dictionnaire Universel de Commerce* (1723), I, col. 965, article, " Commerce de Hollande."

[84] *State Papers of John Thurloe,* VII, 652.

[85] Bodleian Library, Clarendon MS. 83, f. 104, Henry Coventry, Stockholm, to the Earl of Clarendon, April 19, 1665. (Copy)

tions to press for a suspension of arms. His master hoped, he told Pomponne, " that the intentions of this warre was not utterly to ruine but to chastise the dutch, that the interests of sweden and holland were so linked together upon severall accounts but chiefly that of commerce, as upon the ruine of the one that of the other would inevitably follow." [86]

Denmark was entangled even more completely than Sweden in the tentacles of Dutch commercial capitalism, and the kings of Denmark were humiliated by restrictions imposed by the States General in respect to the Sound and Norway tolls. Nevertheless, when confronted with an opportunity to strike a blow at the power whose prevalence they had so hotly denounced, Danish ministers hesitated and, in a Dutch metaphor, began to pour water in their wine. Like the Swedes they did not want to see the Dutch too badly beaten. In part this sprang from political misgivings: " Yet I find apparently," wrote Sir Gilbert Talbot in 1665, " that both the North Crownes discover a great care and concerne that Holland be not depressed to much for they feare least England should be the sole Lord and Master of the Sea and noe power remayne to ballance it." [87] But there were economic misgivings too. Frederick III explained " that all his subjects are ruined if theyre commerce be obstructed with Holland, for in that case, noe part of his dominions can afford him anything: his woods and other commodityes of Norway, and his corne and cattle in Zeland and Holstein will all lye dead upon his hands." [88]

With even greater conviction the Rhine princes identified the prosperity of Dutch trade with the prosperity of their own cities and the improvement of their revenues. On one occasion they administered a stiff rebuke to Hamburg and Bremen for presuming to vie with the power which, the princes asserted, had sheltered and defended Hanseatic trade.[89]

[86] Public Record Office, State Papers, foreign, France 137, f. 184, Sir William Lockhart from the Camp at Alnoy to the Earl of Arlington, June 25/July 5, 1673.

[87] Ibid., State Papers, foreign, Denmark 17, f. 459, To Secretary Bennet, Oct. 28, 1665.

[88] Ibid., Denmark 17, f. 314, Sir Gilbert Talbot to Secretary Bennet, April 15, 1665.

[89] E. Gothein, " Rheinische Zollkongresse und Handelsprojekte am Ende des 17. Jahrhunderts," *Beitrage zur Geschichte vornehmlich Kölns und der Rheinlande, Festschrift für Gustav v. Mevissen* (Köln, 1895), pp. 363, 369 ff.

CHAPTER VI

LOANS AND INVESTMENTS ABROAD

It is when we turn from the uses of Dutch capital in trade to the export of capital in the forms of loans and investments that the extent of capitalism radiating from Amsterdam may best be surmised. As Antwerp had been the center of international finance in the sixteenth century, so was Amsterdam in the seventeenth, and a procession of royal borrowers applied thither with varying success. Public loans to foreign princes or states for political purposes need not detain us, except to notice that it is not always easy to draw a line between public and private lending. Thus the loan of f. 248,000 at 7 per cent to the Elector of Brandenburg in 1616 was nominally made by the receiver general of the Amsterdam Admiralty, Pieter Martensz. Hoeffijser, but the funds were drawn from the customs receipts of that admiralty. On the other hand, the failure of the electoral government to repay the loan would seem to have been partly responsible for the bankruptcy of Hoeffijser in 1641.[1] Another illustration of the close relation between public and private loans concerns Sweden's dependence on the money market of Amsterdam. The States General had lent Gustavus Adolphus rd. 400,000 for the ransom of the fortress of Elfsborg from the Danes. Since the king could not find the interest on this sum, Louis de Geer undertook to pay it, and in 1618 a consortium of Amsterdammers of which he was one, engaged to pay principal and interest of the last instalment of the Elfsborg loan still owing the States General.[2] Sometimes loans made by private capitalists were guaranteed by the States General, as in the case of the quicksilver loans to the emperor negotiated with the Amsterdam house of

[1] Aitzema, I, 259 ff., XI, 657 ff., 673; Rijks Archief, Resolutiën Staten Generaal, CXVIII, f. 215 v., March 26, 1679; J. G. van Dillen, "Geld- en Bankwezen te Amsterdam in de Zeventiende Eeuw," *Zeven Eeuwen Amsterdam,* ed. D'Ailly, II, 142.

[2] E. W. Dahlgren, *Louis de Geers Brev,* p. 14, no. 11; pp. 25 ff., no. 14; pp. 39-40, no. 23; pp. 44 ff., nos. 27-28; Breedvelt-Van Veen, *Louis de Geer,* pp. 48 ff.

Deutz in 1695 and 1698.[3] In 1701 the tsar's ministers reproached the States General with clandestine encouragement of private credits to Sweden.[4] Because the relation between public policy and private capital was intimate, the States General did not neglect to extort commercial advantages from debtor governments, an insistence particularly evident in their financial arrangements with such weak, insolvent states as Denmark, Portugal, and the empire. The attitude may be sufficiently illustrated by a suggestion from Willem Boreel, an experienced diplomat, as to how Portugal's indebtedness might be usefully exploited. "If by the last peace treaties the king of Portugal remains debtor to their High Mightinesses for some sum payable in money or goods, their High Mightinesses might obtain from the king in return, the revenue from the duty on salt at Setubal, thereby reducing the debt and giving an advantage to Netherlands salt-carriers."[5]

For the most part foreign governments seeking credit for purchases, or short-term advances, addressed themselves to private capital in Amsterdam. Richelieu's agents, Jan and Mattheus Hoeufft, were well known in capitalist circles in that city. Jan Hoeufft was one of the projectors of an Amsterdam consortium to monopolize Russian grain exports, and both Hoeuffts invested in the ambitious copper monopoly of 1634.[6] Purchases of naval supplies, ships, and munitions ordered by Richelieu, and monies raised there for the payment of troops or other purposes, were in part financed on credits obtained

[3] Srbik, *Der staatliche Exporthandel Österreichs*, pp. 241, 251; Van Dillen, "Geld- en Bankwezen te Amsterdam," *Zeven Eeuwen Amsterdam*, II, 143.

[4] C. C. Uhlenbeck, *Verslag aangaande een Onderzoek in de Archieven van Rusland*, p. 74. Sometimes political influence was used to prevent a loan by private capital. Thus in 1651 the Vroedschap resolved to discourage "op de stilste maniere" any advances by Amsterdam capitalists to the king of Denmark on the security of the payments to be made by the States General according to the Redemption Treaty. (Gemeente Archief, Vroedschapsresolutiën, XIX, f. 188, Nov. 8, 1651)

[5] *Brieven . . . Johan de Witt*, I, 630, April 19, 1663. (Translation.) It is odd that Boreel did not know of the treaty of 1661 with Portugal by which the States General had secured almost exactly the arrangement he had suggested, though the profits were allocated to the West India Company rather than to the salt traders. (Aitzema, X, 119-120.)

[6] J. E. Elias, "Contract tot Oprichting van een Zweedsch Factorie-comptoir te Amsterdam in 1663," *Bijdragen*, XXIV, 361-362; Van Dillen, "Amsterdamsche Notarieele Acten betreffende den Koperhandel," *ibid.*, LVIII, p. 220.

by Jan Hoeufft. We find De Geer grumbling because Hoeufft was slow in paying for arms supplied on credit.[7] There is fragmentary evidence to show that later bankers to the French crown—Herinx, Samuel Bernard, and Jean-Henri Huguetan—were accustomed to apply to Amsterdam for credits; and that Amsterdam's complaisance was not refused in years when there was war between France and the republic.[8] It was with the assistance of Amsterdam that Colbert raised the sum required for the purchase of Dunkirk from Charles II.[9]

Philip Burlamachi, who for about twenty years acted as financial agent or ' factor ' of James I and Charles I of England, performing much the same kinds of services that occupied Hoeufft in France, like Hoeufft had correspondents in Amsterdam. Chief of these was his brother-in-law, Philip Calandrini, but he had other business friends in that city: Paulo Pels, Pieter and Charles de Latfeur, and John Quarles of the Fellowship of Merchant Adventurers. Though Burlamachi called himself ' merchant,' his energies were almost entirely absorbed in the gruelling business of finding credit for the pressing needs of the crown, paying out the monies thus raised, and fulfilling a variety of commissions for his royal master which ranged from buying works of art, to raising, transporting, and paying troops. Since the Stuarts, like most kings, were laggard debtors, and since most of Burlamachi's activities were not of a kind to bring in a constant income, one wonders where he got the large sums advanced in repeated loans to the crown, for instance the £70,000 which

[7] Dahlgren, pp. 119, 124. On Richelieu's dependence on Hoeufft as banker, see *Correspondance Inédite du Comte d'Avaux avec son Père . . . (1627-1642)*, ed. A. Boppe (Paris, 1887), p. 117, note. Lopez too made advances to the French crown to pay for ships and war *matériel* purchased by him in Amsterdam and other towns of Holland, which suggests that some part of the credits were raised there. *(Lettres, Instructions Diplomatiques et Papiers d'État du Cardinal de Richelieu*, ed. Avenel, VII, 303.) On Hoeufft and Lopez, above pp. 30 n., 38 n., and further mention of Hoeufft, below, p. 121.

[8] On Herinx's contacts with Amsterdam, see the letter referred to in the note next following; for those of Bernard, Victor de Swarte, *Un Banquier du trésor royal au xviii ᵉ siècle: Samuel Bernard . . .* (Paris, 1893), pp. 31 ff., 53; and for those of Huguetan: André-E. Sayous, " Le Financier Jean-Henri Huguetan à Amsterdam et à Genève," *Bulletin de la Société d'Histoire et d'Archéologie de Genève* (1937), VI, pp. 255 ff.

[9] *Correspondance Administrative sous le Règne de Louis XIV*, ed. Depping, III, 10-11.

he raised singlehanded in 1625 [10]—probably by juggling his credit and that of his friends in London, Amsterdam, Rouen, and perhaps elsewhere. On one occasion when money on which he had counted for repayment was withheld from him, he wrote warningly to Secretary Conway: " I say to your excellency in confidence and frankly that if the means of paying the bills of exchange drawn by my Amsterdam friends be taken from me, their power and mine of serving his Majesty will be taken." [11] It was through Burlamachi and Calandrini that Amsterdam helped to finance Buckingham's ill-fated wars with loans for which the duke's jewels and certain others belonging to the crown, were security.[12] Burlamachi's patent for the export of iron ordnance was exploited in association with Elias Trip, the great munitions merchant of Amsterdam.[13] We find Burlamachi's name among those of the ' merchant strangers ' arrested and tried in 1619 on a charge of having exported coin, presumably to Holland.[14] When he failed in 1633, he was deeply in debt to Calandrini and other Amsterdam creditors, as well as to certain merchants of London.

All parties to the English civil wars sought credit, as they sought arms, in Amsterdam. In 1642 the crown jewels once more travelled to Holland, this time in the hands of Queen Henrietta Maria, who pawned them to various persons in

[10] Public Record Office, State Papers, domestic 16/25, no. 108.   " The humble petition of Philip Burlamachi of London Marchant [April] 1626." A few years later the crown owed Burlamachi and his friends £128,573. (*Calendar of State Papers, domestic series, 1629-1631,* ed. John Bruce [London, 1860], p. 147.) There is an account of this active and enterprising man by A. V. Judges, " Philip Burlamachi, a Financier of the Thirty Years' War," *Economica* (1926), VI, 285; and abundant data about him in the *Calendar of State Papers, domestic series,* from 1608 to 1644. For other mentions him in this monograph, see above, p. 30 and below, p. 123 n.

[11] *"Je dis a V.E. en confiance et librement que si on m'oste le moyen de payer les lettres de change de mes amis d'Amsterdam on ostera a eux et a moy le moyen de servir Sa M^{te}."* (Public Record Office, State Papers, domestic, 16/10, no. 65, Nov. 1625.)

[12] The somewhat shabby adventures of these jewels in Amsterdam in the years 1625-1636 may be followed in the volumes of the *Calendar of State Papers, domestic series,* covering those years. Both Burlamachi and his brother-in-law, Philip Calandrini of Amsterdam, were involved in these transactions.

[13] *Calendar of State Papers, domestic series, Addenda, 1580-1625,* ed. M. A. E. Green (London, 1872), pp. 629-630; *ibid., 1623-1625* (London, 1859), p. 463; *ibid., 1631-1633,* ed. John Bruce (London, 1862), pp. 435, 443.

[14] See below, p. 123.

Amsterdam, Rotterdam, and the Hague in order to obtain funds for the purchase of arms for the royal cause.[15] At almost the same time the Committee of Both Kingdoms was seeking a loan of £300,000 from Holland to finance the parliamentary armies.[16] The parliament of Scotland also borrowed in the Netherlands, and earlier the Covenanters had managed to buy arms on credit.[17] We have seen that the Prince of Orange used his own credit in Amsterdam to raise money for the exiled English king.[18] On his restoration Charles II suggested a loan of £2,000,000 to a member of the States General's embassy of congratulation, the sum to be paid off in two years. The ambassador at first assumed that Amsterdam would be agreeable, but renewal of the Navigation Act, and a bill to exclude the Dutch from British coastal fisheries which was passed by the House of Commons, convinced the city that the king could not be made serviceable to his creditors.[19]

Neither branch of the House of Austria could command much credit in Amsterdam unless supported by valuable considerations, but these insolvent monarchies had assets of no small interest to Amsterdam capitalists. Mention has already

---

[15] On this, as on the earlier occasion, the men with money to lend doubted whether the king could legally make "a good pawn" of crown property. Finally the jewels were pledged in small parcels to various persons in Amsterdam, Rotterdam, and the Hague, at sums below their real value, and were lost when the queen was no longer able to pay the interest. Brugmans, "Handel en Nijverheid," *Amsterdam in de Zeventiende Eeuw,* II, 33; Carola Oman, *Henrietta Maria* (New York, 1936), pp. 128 ff., *Calendar of State Papers, domestic series, 1644,* ed. William Douglas Hamilton (London, 1888), p. 259; *ibid., 1644-1645* (London, 1890), pp. 387-388, 440, 448, 470, 501.

[16] *Acts and Ordinances of the Interregnum, 1642-1660 . . . ,* eds. C. H. Firth and R. S. Rait . . . (3 vols., London, 1911), I, 70, 193, 220-221; *Calendar of State Papers, domestic series, 1644,* p. 68.

[17] Public Record Office, State Papers, foreign, Holland 84/219 (a bundle of odds and ends whose eventual arrangement had not been determined when I examined it), Translation of a memorial from the Dutch ambassadors, Beverwaert, Van Hoorn, and Van Gogh, dated June 12/22, [1661], in behalf of Adriaen and Cornelis Lampsins of Flushing who in 1644 had guaranteed debts contracted in the Netherlands by the Parliament of Scotland. On these brothers Lampsins, see Elias, *De Vroedschap van Amsterdam,* II, 976. On credits to Covenanters: Clarendon, *The History of the Rebellion and Civil Wars in England,* I, 70.

[18] Above, p. 55.

[19] See the correspondence between Louis de Beverwaert and De Witt on this subject, Sept. 14-Oct. 15, 1660. (*Brieven . . . Johan de Witt,* IV, 25, 37.)

been made of the quicksilver monopoly. In 1659 the emperor obtained the first of a succession of advances from Johan Deutz of Amsterdam, security for which was the exclusive factorage in northern Europe of quicksilver from the Idrian mines. This profitable monopoly was much coveted in capitalistic circles in Amsterdam, but the house of Deutz was to continue in possession for almost a century. The influence of Deutz's brother-in-law, Johan de Witt, Pensionary of Holland, had been exerted to secure the original contract. Thereafter the imperial government could never shake off the debt, which in 1695 was increased by the handsome sum of f. 1,550,000.[20] In financing the factorage and the loans it was the practice of Deutz to borrow the required funds at 4 per cent and lend them to the emperor at 6.[21] In 1664 an attempt on the part of the imperial government to raise another loan in Amsterdam on the security of unmortgaged Habsburg properties failed, and the imperial jewels were pawned to certain Portuguese residents of the city.[22] In 1700 the output of the Hungarian copper mines was pledged to the heirs of Deutz.[23]

Of great financial interest to Amsterdam was the contract (*asiento*) for supplying Negro slaves to the Spanish colonies in America. Curaçao, occupied by the Dutch West India Company in 1634, became a staple point where Negroes transported by the company were delivered to agents of the *asientistas* or to planters who ventured on a contraband trade. It is significant that the Amsterdam chamber of the company which furnished most of the capital for the slave trade attempted to establish a claim to Curaçao exclusive of the other

[20] Srbik, *passim;* Elias, II, 630 ff.; *Brieven aan Johan de Witt*, eds. Fruin and Japikse, II, 172-173. The loan of 1695 would seem to have been made ostensibly by the States General to the emperor, but the security was that supply of quicksilver already in the hands of the Widow Deutz and Son, and that to be consigned to them later, and it is evident that the whole transaction was to go through their hands, the States General guaranteeing payment of interest if the emperor should default. Gemeente Oud-Archief, Arch. Burgem., Lands- en Gewestelijk-bestuur, Stukken Buitenlandsche Zaken, W. 1-10. Printed text of the contract between the States General and the emperor.

[21] Srbik, p. 32. This had likewise been the practice of Deutz's predecessor in the factorage, Abondio Inzaghi. *Ibid.,* p. 31.

[22] *Ibid.,* p. 26.

[23] *Ibid.,* pp. 263 ff.

chambers.[24] In the second half of the century Amsterdam seems to have been the business headquarters of the slave trade, and contracts for deliveries of Negroes were drawn up there.[25] Successive holders of the *asiento,* though they bought slaves of English and Portuguese companies, depended in the main on the Dutch West India Company for supplies. Relations with the Genoese asientists, Grillo and Lomelino, who obtained the contract in 1662, and with their successors, Garcia and Silvio, from 1675, were so close that Dr. van Brakel has suggested the capital for acquisition of the *asiento* may have been put up in Amsterdam.[26] Especially concerned in the West India Company's business with the asientists was the Amsterdam house of Jean Coymans and Co., whose representative at Cadiz was Balthazar Coymans, brother of Jean Coymans. In 1685 when the incumbent then in possession of the *asiento* was in financial difficulties, Balthazar Coymans succeeded in ousting him, and won the contract for himself and his company from the Council of the Indies. The cash payment of 200,000 crowns to the Spanish government, an indispensable feature of the bargain, was furnished by the Amsterdam house of Coymans. But the success of Balthazar Coymans soon aroused religious and patriotic scruples against allowing this lucrative and soul-saving business to fall into the hands of a Dutch heretic. The Inquisition made the annulment of the contract a matter of conscience, and though Coymans was willing to sign an engagement to establish Catholic missionaries in the West India Company's factories in Guinea, his *asiento* was quashed in 1689.[27] This did not mean, however, the end of

---

[24] S. van Brakel, "Bescheiden over den Slavenhandel der West-Indische Compagnie," *Economisch-historisch Jaarboek* (1918), IV, 54, note.

[25] *Ibid.,* pp. 47 ff., G. W. Kernkamp, "Een Contract tot Slavenhandel van 1657," *Bijdragen en Mededeelingen* (1901), XXII, 444 ff.; A.-E. Sayous, "Le Rôle d'Amsterdam dans l'Histoire du Capitalisme," *Revue Historique,* CLXXXIII, 273; Georges Scelle, *La Traite Négrière,* I, 480 ff.; II, 119 ff.; Irene A. Wright, "The Coymans Asiento, 1685-1689," *Bijdragen voor Vaderlandsche Geschiedenis en Oudheidkunde* (1924), 6th ser., I, 23 ff.; *Journal of the House of Commons,* VII, 741, July 30, 1659, Abstract of letters received from Jamaica from the commander-in-chief, written April 20, 1659. See also, two remonstrances from the directors of the West India Company concerning interruptions to this trade, Nov. 14, 1668, and Nov. 14, 1680, Rijks Archief, Resolutiën Staten Generaal, XCVII, f. 366v.-367; CXXI, f. 315.

[26] Van Brakel, *Economisch-historisch Jaarboek,* IV, 52.

[27] Wright, *Bijdragen,* pp. 23 ff.

Amsterdam's participation in the slave trade. In 1698, under
cover of the Portuguese company then holding the *asiento*,
certain Jewish correspondents of that company in Amsterdam
were negotiating with the West India Company for consignments of Negroes.[28]

In a succession of wars between the northern crowns for
supremacy in the Baltic, Dutch capital, like Dutch shipping,
fought on both sides. When Louis de Geer in 1618 assumed responsibility for paying the interest on the loan by
the States General to the Swedish king, Gustavus Adolphus,
he opened a long, intricate chapter of financial commitments
which were to continue throughout his life and into the lives
of his heirs. He made repeated loans, advanced credit for
long or short periods, made payments for the Swedish government both in Sweden and abroad, armed and equipped Swedish
armies, and like Hoeufft in France and Burlamachi in England,
carried out a variety of commissions for the court. These
loans and advances, along with his arms business and industrial enterprises, eventually required his naturalization and
residence in Sweden, though he continued to make long so-
journs in Amsterdam in the interest of his affairs. His most
famous exploit was the assembling, chartering, and equipping
of a naval squadron in Amsterdam to serve Sweden against
Denmark in 1645. When it returned badly mauled by the
Danish fleet, he managed to reform, refit, supplement, and
send it out again, this time to better success. De Geer claimed
to have spent more than f. 1,400,000 on these expeditions.[29]
The capital employed by him in Sweden represented, at least
in the early stages of his career, not only his own mounting
fortune, but also contributions of Amsterdam associates who
entrusted their funds to him. Because of the slender resources
of the Swedish monarchy, repayment presented a complex
problem. De Geer's claims were settled by consignments of
copper, by leases and grants of crown lands, by allocations of
customs duties in Swedish ports, and by sundry privileges and
exemptions. A patent of nobility was one consideration.[30]

[28] Scelle, II, 119-120.
[29] On this episode: Breedvelt-Van Veen, pp. 153 ff. G. W. Kernkamp,
De Sleutels van de Sont ('s-Gravenhage, 1890), pp. 60 ff.
[30] Breedvelt-Van Veen, pp. 132 ff.; Dahlgren, *Louis de Geer*, II, 285 ff.

Elias Trip, De Geer's sometime partner, sometime competitor in the arms trade, also became involved in Swedish finance, partly in consequence of deliveries of arms on credit, and partly as a result of the monopoly of Swedish copper exports which he had consummated by 1629. In 1635 his claims against the Swedish crown amounted to f. 864,048.[31] Although the stock of copper in his hands was sufficient to cover most of this debt, we find his heirs insisting in 1682 that the Swedish government still owed " many hundred thousand gulden " to his estate.[32]

In De Geer's time and later there were other Amsterdammers seeking their fortunes in Sweden. There was the group formed by Samuel Blommaert, of which Mattheus Hoeufft was a member, to exploit a privilege gained from the Swedish crown to establish a brass factory at Nacka.[33] There were the younger De Geers and Trips who succeeded to the property rights and so to the financial responsibilities of their fore-runners.[34] There were the Momma brothers who opened copper mines in Swedish Lapland and farmed the property and reve-nues retained by Queen Christina after her abdication.[35] There were the four Amsterdam merchants, Baack, Graafland, Hulft and Duysent, who in 1663 succeeded in obtaining a monopoly of the export of iron guns to the Netherlands.[36] Concessions such as these required financial persuasions to secure, as well as capital to exploit.

The money market of Amsterdam was slower to respond to the needs of the Danish crown, but in the Danish period of the Thirty Years' War, Paul de Willem of Amsterdam found or furnished credit for arms for the Danish forces, and in 1626 Louis de Geer extended credit for munitions

---

[31] Van Dillen, "Amsterdamsche Notarieele Acten betreffende den Koper-handel," *Bijdragen,* LVIII, 219.

[32] Rijks Archief, Resolutiën Staten Generaal, CXXV, f. 14, July 6, 1682.

[33] Breedvelt-Van Veen, p. 115; Dahlgren, *Louis de Geer,* II, 401.

[34] Elias, *Bijdragen,* XXIV, 374 ff. See also, above, p. 37.

[35] Elias, *Bijdragen,* XXIV, 378; Dahlgren, II, 386. There is an interesting sketch of the Momma brothers by Pomponne in a letter to Colbert from Stockholm, Sept. 17, 1667. *(Correspondance Administrative sous le règne de Louis XIV,* ed. Depping, III, 406.)

[36] Elias, *Bijdragen,* XXIV, 383 ff.; and by the same author: *De Vroedschap van Amsterdam,* I, 317, 524, 533.

then desperately needed by the defeated Danes.[37] The following year the Amsterdam firm of Jacques de Mares and Co. lent
Christian IV f. 150,000.[38] After the States General became
alarmed by the rapid advance of Swedish power in the Baltic,
Amsterdam capital, following the trend of foreign policy,
became more interested in Denmark and Norway. A position
curiously paralleling that of the De Geer and Trip dynasties
in Sweden, was attained in Denmark by another family of
southern Netherlands origin, the Marcelises. The first Gabriel
Marcelis had settled in Hamburg, and from there formed
business ties in Amsterdam and Copenhagen. In 1641 his
son of the same name became commissioner of Christian IV
in Amsterdam, and thereafter played an active role in the
commercial and financial affairs of the Danish kingdom. Celio
Marcelis, brother of this second Gabriel, after a turbulent
career in Amsterdam as exporter of munitions under suspicion
of engaging in contraband trade, moved to Denmark, where
he made himself indispensable to the Danish government in
the capacities of economic adviser, government contractor
(suspected of malfeasance), mining entrepreneur, munitions
merchant, timber exporter, and banker.[39] In 1645 Gabriel hired
and armed an auxiliary squadron in Amsterdam to assist the
Danish fleet, as De Geer was doing at the same time, in the
same place, and for the same war, in behalf of Sweden.[40] In
the crisis of 1658-1659, when Copenhagen was besieged by the
Swedish army, the brothers raised rd. 52,000 for the maintenance of the garrison, and Celio himself took part in the defense of the city.[41] There were other loans: one by Gabriel
Marcelis to Frederick III for rd. 450,406 secured on tolls
and copper tithes.[42] This may be the one referred to by his
heirs in 1681, when they claimed that he had furnished very

[37] Breedvelt-Van Veen, p. 75, note; *Baltische Archivalia*, ed. G. W. Kernkamp (Rijks Geschiedkundige Publicatiën, kleine serie, Vol. IV, 's-Gravenhage,
1909), p. 82.
[38] *Ibid.*, p. 77.
[39] M. G. de Boer, "Een Amsterdamsche ' Lorrendraaier,' " *Jaarboek*,
XXXVIII, 37 ff.; Elias, *De Vroedschap van Amsterdam*, II, 871 ff.; G. W.
Kernkamp, *De Sleutels van de Sont*, pp. 291 ff.
[40] G. W. Kernkamp, *De Sleutels*, pp. 60, 91, 294-295.
[41] De Boer, *Jaarboek*, XXXVIII, 64-65; Kernkamp, *Baltische Archivalia*,
p. 93.
[42] *Ibid.*

notable and large sums of money to the crown of Denmark, not only out of his own funds, but many thousands from other inhabitants of this country, even from widows and orphans, as well as sums taken up from merchants on credit." [43] In 1666 we hear of a contract for arms to be supplied to Denmark, negotiated by Gabriel Marcelis with his brothers-in-law, Samuel Sautijn and Pieter Trip.[44] Again like De Geer in Sweden, the Marcelis brothers became possessors of great estates in Denmark and Norway.[45]

The Danish crown found other creditors in Amsterdam. Prominent among them was Joachim Irgens, Holsteiner by birth but Amsterdammer by adoption, who had bought a fine house on the Keizersgracht in 1652, and had married into the wealthy Bicker family. He had opened copper mines near Trondhyem in 1646, which implies some form of cash or credit transaction. In 1657 Irgens and his associates made a loan of rd. 60,000 to the Danish government, one consideration being the right to export copper from Irgens' Norwegian mines free of duty and exempt from the royal right of pre-emption.[46] Evidently this was only one of several transactions of the kind, for Irgens' widow asserted in 1681 that " her husband during his lifetime had advanced large sums to the king of Denmark in times of war as also at other times, and that her husband had not only employed his own funds therein, but also many thousands from other persons in the city of Amsterdam, taken up from merchants, widows and orphans, for which he had pledged his own person and goods." [47] As a natural sequel to the credit relation Irgens became one of the greatest landed proprietors in the two kingdoms, with an estate on the island of Zealand accounted worth rd. 130,000, crown lands in Jutland and Norway for

[43] Rijks Archief, Resolutiën Staten Generaal, CXXIII, f. 40v., July 12, 1681.
[44] Kernkamp, *Baltische Archivalia,* pp. 60, 66.
[45] *Ibid.* pp. 92 ff.
[46] Rijks Archief, Staten Generaal, Lias Denemarken 5910, Petition of Joachim Irgens and Co., July 13, 1656; *ibid.,* 5913. Entry of a letter from the States General to the king of Denmark, June 5, 1660. For an account of Irgens, see Elias, *De Vroedschap van Amsterdam,* I, 347.
[47] Rijks Archief, Resolutiën Staten Generaal, CXXII, 339 v., April 25, 1681. (Translation.) The reference to widows and orphans by the heirs of both Irgens and Gabriel Marcelis probably means that both had borrowed from the Orphans' Chamber (*Weeskamer*) of Amsterdam.

which he had paid the king rd. 100,000, and the copper mines reported to bring in rd. 25,000 to 30,000 annually.[48]

A vociferous creditor was Sir William Davidson, a Scot by birth but long domiciled in Amsterdam, whose claims against the Danish crown and court amounted in 1668 by his own arithmetic to rd. 96,000, but only about a sixth of this had been lent to the king; the rest had been advanced to persons at court, or represented Davidson's one-third interest in the Danish Salt Company. In the course of these transactions Sir William had acquired lands, iron-works, and sawmills in Norway. The remaining capital in the salt monopoly would seem to have been contributed in whole or in greater part by Amsterdam.[49] One-third interest was held by Jonas Trellund, Danish by birth, but Amsterdammer by choice, and the remaining third by Cort Adelaar, the Danish admiral. Both Trellund and Adelaar had married into the rich Pelt famiy, who supplied or enlisted Amsterdam capital to launch this enterprise. Trellund also found investors in Amsterdam who were ready to participate in the commercial exploitation of Iceland, for which he with others had secured a patent.[50] The brothers Gillis and Willem Sautijn were interested in Iceland too, and in 1665 contracted with a Danish patentee for the exclusive right to export sulphur from Iceland.[51] One could add several Amsterdam names to this list of investors in Denmark and Danish dependencies, but the pattern has been sufficiently indicated.

Russia's wealth of undeveloped resources attracted such a swarm of Dutch concessionaires that the States General felt compelled to protest against the exclusive privileges obtained by some few of their subjects at the expense of the many.[52]

[48] *Ibid.,* Staten Generaal, Lias Denemarken 5919, Le Maire to the States General [April,] 1672.

[49] W. del Court, "Sir William Davidson in Nederland (1668)," *Bijdragen voor Vaderlandsche Geschiedenis en Oudheidkunde* (1906), 4th ser., V, 375 ff., and especially pp. 406 ff., 420 ff.; Gemeente Oud-Archief, Not. Arch. 3410, Notaris Philips Engebrecht, entries of June 4 and 7, 1666.

[50] For Trellund and his connections with Adelaar and with the Pelt family: Marie Simon Thomas, *Onze Ijslandsvaarders in de 17de en 18de Eeuw* (Amsterdam, 1935), *passim,* and especially pp. 60 ff., 91 ff., 122 ff.

[51] *Ibid.,* p. 133; Rijks Archief, Resolutiën Staten Generaal, XCVII, 400 v., Nov. 27, 1668.

[52] *Ibid.,* Staten Generaal, Lias Rusland, 66-7, Articles proposed by the Russian ambassadors, June 28, 1647.

A form of investment highly congenial to Amsterdam was the farming of the tsar's export monopolies, which ranged from small but lucrative trifles, such as caviare and isinglass, to some of Russia's most important commodities, as tar, hemp, leathers, train-oil, linseed, salmon, and wool. Further opportunities lay in the handling of government contracts for military supplies and imported luxuries. This business was largely in the hands of a few prominent Amsterdam merchants who had succeeded in getting themselves enrolled among the *gosti* (purveyors to the court), and who vied with one another for the privileges and immunities to be inserted in their *genadebrieven,* and for the favor of favorites at court.[53]

Elsewhere in Europe we have glimpses of Amsterdammers ensconced in advantageous positions which called for some capital investment. In the years 1618-1621, and possibly later, Hollanders were farming the king of Poland's mint.[54] The customs of the Canary Islands were farmed by a group of Amsterdam Jews in association with co-religionists in Rouen.[55] The republic of Venice contracted a debt to Samuel Sautijn, father of the Sautijn brothers mentioned above, but whether the principal represented a loan, or arms or goods sold on credit, we cannot be sure.[56] In 1658 we find Amsterdammers combining with Tuscans to obtain a patent for the sole right to export caviare from Russia, Italy being the only foreign market for this comestible.[57] The most imposing intrusion of

[53] On Russo-Dutch commercial relations in this period see, besides the works cited above, p. 39, note 103, Boris Raptschinsky, "Uit de Geschiedenis van den Amsterdamschen Handel op Rusland in de XVIIᵉ Eeuw," *Jaarboek Amstelodamum* (1937), XXXIV, pp. 57 ff.

[54] *Calendar of State Papers, domestic series, 1619-1623,* ed. Green (London, 1858), p. 211.

[55] Rijks Archief, Staten Generaal, Lias Spagnien 6759, copy of an undated minute possibly by the Spanish ambassador, Antoine Brun.

[56] A brief account of this family of merchant bankers is given by Elias, *De Vroedschap van Amsterdam,* II, 573 ff. It was to obtain repayment of this loan that Sautijn was endeavoring in 1670 to have sequestered funds belonging to Venice in the bank of Amsterdam. (Gemeente Oud-Archief, Diplom. Missiven, Engeland 3, Van Beuningen to the Burgomasters of Amsterdam, July 19, 1670; Rijks Archief, Resolutiën Staten Generaal, XCVII, f. 476, Dec. 21, 1668).

[57] In the first half of this century the English Muscovy Company and Dutch merchants had vied for this patent which, in the opinion of an English merchant returned a certain profit of from 30 to 40 per cent a year. (Public Record Office, State Papers, foreign, Russia 3, f. 118 v., June 25, 1666.) In

Amsterdam capitalism in Italy was the marble monopoly built up by Gillis and Willem Sautijn and Pieter van der Straten, consul at Livorno. They acquired sole right to export certain kinds of marble from the territories of the republic of Genoa, of the duke of Massa, and of the grand duke of Tuscany.[58] This explains why " There are such vast Magazines in Amsterdam, that a Man would think . . . there were Quarries of Marble near the City Gates," and why marbles for Louis XIV's palace at Versailles were bought in Amsterdam.[59]

When debtors princely or private defaulted, as so often happened, creditors were wont to tighten their grip on the collateral. It is not always clear whether a particular loan or advance was made for the sake of the properties pledged, or the properties taken over because no other form of recovery was possible. The Marcelises complained that they had been compelled to accept lands in settlement of debts owing them by the Danish crown, and offered to surrender their real properties for a fraction of the principal sum.[60] Irgens too had been repaid in lands, willy-nilly.[61] When the king of Denmark demanded an oath of allegiance of all landowners in his kingdom, the Dutch resident advised the States General that

1658 John Hebdon, then the tsar's commissioner in Amsterdam, made over the patent to the Amsterdam and Livorno house of Isaack Jan Nijs *cum sociis.* (Van Zuiden, *Bijdrage tot de Kennis van de Hollandsch-Russische Relaties,* p. 12, and bijlage iii, pp. 38 ff.; Bodleian Library, Clarendon MS 85, f. 80, Sir John Finch, Leghorn, to the Earl of Clarendon, April 1/11, 1667.) In the second half of this century this small but pleasing monopoly seems to have remained in Dutch hands. Scheltema, *Rusland en de Nederlanden,* I, 284; " Mémoire touchant le négoce et la navigation des hollandois," ed. Blok, *Bijdragen,* XXIV, 244; Johann Georg Korb, *Diary of an Austrian Secretary of Legation at the Court of Czar Peter the Great,* ed. Count Mac-Donnell (2 vols., London, 1863), II, 147.

[58] " Pietro van der Straten a Dutch merchant hath lately procured a pattent from the Great Duke, as hee had formerly at Massa and Genova, about Paveing marbles, soe it seemes those sorts ought to be bought of him, hee pretends to afford them cheaper then what is agreed for at Carrera." (Public Record Office, State Papers, foreign, Tuscany 7, Thomas Dethick, Livorno, to Joseph Williamson, Nov. 4/14, 1667.) On this patent and the participation of the brothers Sautijn, see Brugmans, " Handel en Nijverheid," *Amsterdam in de Zeventiende Eeuw,* II, 93, note.

[59] *A Description of Holland . . . by an English Gentleman* (1701), pp. 17-18.

[60] Kernkamp, *Baltische Archivalia,* pp. 92 ff.; Rijks Archief, Resolutiën Staten Generaal, CXXIII, f. 41; Robert Molesworth, *An Account of Denmark,* p. 80; J. C., *Denmark vindicated,* p. 205.

[61] Elias, *De Vroedschap van Amsterdam,* I, 347.

this would embarrass many of their High Mightinesses' subjects who had taken over real estate because they were unable to collect their debts in any other forms.[62]

By whatever order of causation a large number of farms, concessions, and monopolies, particularly in the countries of the North, fell into Dutch hands, and those hands undertook to make them productive. Where Dutch capital went, there swamps were drained, mines opened, forests exploited, canals constructed, ships built, new industries established, mills turned, and trading companies were organized. The economic life of the Scandinavian countries was honeycombed by Dutch enterprise, and many of their most valuable resources were appropriated by the invaders.[63] " It may be said," observed Huet about the year 1694, " that the Dutch are in some respects masters of the commerce of the Swedish kingdom since they are masters of the copper trade. The farmers of these mines, being always in need of money, and not finding any in Sweden, pledge this commodity to merchants of Amsterdam who advance them the necessary funds. It is the same with tar and pitch, certain merchants of Amsterdam having bought the greater part of these farms of the king, and made considerable advances besides, so that the result is these commodities and most others are found as cheap in Amsterdam as in Sweden."[64] " The copper mines in Norway . . .," Savary had said in 1675, " belong in part to the estate of the treasurer of the king of Denmark, and to two merchants of Amsterdam who ordinarily market the product in Hamburg or Amsterdam." [65] Unquestionably the profit-making motive was uppermost in the minds of Amsterdammers who put their money to work in foreign countries, but they were not absentee *rentiers*, nor carpetbaggers

[62] Rijks Archief, Staten Generaal, Lias Denemarken 5917, Dec. 5, 1669.

[63] For the development of Swedish trade and resources by Netherlanders, see Johannes Kretzschmar, " Schwedische Handelscompaniën und Kolonisationsversuche im 16. und 17. Jahrhundert," *Hansische Geschichtsblätter* (1911), XVII, 215 ff.; also the biographies of Louis de Geer by Breedvelt-Van Veen, and Dahlgren, *passim;* Van Dillen, " Amsterdamsche Notarieele Acten betreffende den Koperhandel," *Bijdragen*, LVIII, 211 ff.; Elias, " Contract tot Oprichting van een Zweedsch Factorie-comptoir," *ibid.*, XXIV, 356 ff. A similar spirit of enterprise in Norway and Denmark was exhibited by the Marcelises, by Irgens, and by Sir William Davidson. (See above, pp. 113 ff.)

[64] *Mémoires sur le Commerce des Hollandois*, p. 59. (Translation)

[65] *Le Parfait négociant*, book ii, p. 91. (Translation)

carrying off whatever was transportable. They were capitalist entrepreneurs who raised the commercial and industrial potential of the countries whose resources they developed. An authority on the economic history of Sweden in the seventeenth century has said: " Dutch immigrants dominated almost everything that was new in the economic life of Sweden at that time." [66]

Dutch activities in Russia in this century included—as in Sweden and Norway—pioneer work in iron- and copper-mining, metallurgy, and the manufacture of munitions; also lumbering for export, shipbuilding, and such allied industries as hemp-working and rope-making. The first sawmill, first paper-mill, first powder-mill, and first glass furnace in Russia were Dutch enterprises; so was the first postal service. Less successful were Dutch attempts to initiate cloth and silk manufactures in Russia in this century.[67] It should not surprise us to find among several Dutch ironmasters and purveyors to the court who prospered in Russia, the name of Pieter Marcelis, brother to the second Gabriel and to Celio, whose activities in Denmark and Norway we have noticed.[68] Nor should it surprise us to learn that one of the greatest of Amsterdam's merchant princes in the Muscovy trade in the second half of the century, Coenraet van Klenck, had irons in the fire in Sweden too, where he became a landed proprietor, and was in consequence ennobled.[69] Amsterdam had a long reach and a strong grasp.

England and France offered less virgin soil to foreign capitalism than the countries of the North, the commercial and industrial aptitudes of their own middle classes being vigorous and competitive, and finding aggressive support from their respective governments. But in both countries Dutch capital was at work. In France Dutchmen engaged in the manufacture of pottery, fine cloth, serge, and linen; in dyeing, distilling, sugar-refining, paper-making, glass- and instrument-making, and shipbuilding.[70] How far these enterprises involved invest-

[66] E. F. Hecksher, " The Bank of Sweden in its connection with the Bank of Amsterdam," *History of the Principal Public Banks,* p. 162.

[67] See the works cited in Chap. I, note 103, p. 39, above.

[68] There is much information about Pieter Marcelis's activities in Russia in the first volume of Scheltema's *Rusland en de Nederlanden, passim.*

[69] Elias, *De Vroedschap van Amsterdam,* II, 564 ff.

[70] Mathorez, *Les Étrangers en France sous l'ancien régime,* II, 207 ff.

ments of capital it is impossible to say. Probably almost all were on a small scale. In two industries, sugar-refining and paper-making, we may be sure of Dutch capital. There were Dutch refineries at one or another period in this century in Marseille, Bordeaux, La Rochelle, Angers, Saumur, Orleans, and probably at Nantes.[71] At Angoulême in the mid-seventeenth century a number of Dutch factors handled the export of paper from Rochefort, La Rochelle, and Tonnay. They would rent paper-mills, install a master papermaker, and advance the necessary capital without interest, to be returned at the termination of the contract. One of the most important of these capitalists was Abraham Janssen, who had three mills in Angoumois, presided over by his three brothers. In addition to the output of these mills, Janssen handled paper produced in Limousin and Périgord.[72]

In the draining of marshes in France Netherlanders participated as entrepreneurs, engineers, investors, and finally as settlers on the reclaimed lands. This work was initiated by Humphrey Bradley, Brabançon notwithstanding his name, who had already offered his engineering services in England but found no takers.[73] In 1607 he obtained a patent from Henri IV for a *Société pour le Desséchement des Marais et Lacs de France*, under which privilege a series of drainage undertakings were carried out with varying success in several French provinces. Each of these enterprises was separately financed by a group of entrepreneurs, among whom Netherlanders from both southern and northern provinces bore a conspicuous part. The

[71] *Ibid.*, II, 241 ff.; Malvezin, *Histoire du commerce de Bordeaux*, II, 371-372; Jacob Spon, *Voyage d'Italie, de Dalmatie, de Grèce, et du Levant, fait aux Années 1675 & 1676* (2 vols., Amsterdam, 1679), I, 24; É. Gabory, "La Marine et le Commerce de Nantes," *Annales de Bretagne*, XVII, p. 39. In 1679 one Adriaen Goverts *cum sociis*, all burghers of Amsterdam, were seeking restitution of their one-third property in a sugar-mill in France, which had been seized by French authorities in the war ending in 1678. (Rijks Archief, Resolutiën Staten Generaal, CXIX, f. 285v., Sept. 30, 1679.)

[72] Mathorez, *Les Etrangers*, II, 244; *Dictionnaire Universel de Commerce* (1723), II, 967-968; III (1730), 1051 ff.; [Huet], *Mémoires sur le Commerce des Hollandois*, p. 38; Enschedé, "Papier en Papierhandel in Noord-Nederland," *Tijdschrift voor Boek- en Bibliotheekwezen*, VII, 97 ff., 173 ff., 205 ff.

[73] *Calendar of State Papers, domestic series, 1591-1594*, ed. Green, pp. 334-335, Humfrey Bradley to Lord Burghley, March 29, 1593. It is noteworthy that Bradley offered to induce "certain gentlemen of wealth" to put up the capital necessary for draining the fens.

greatest investor and sustaining pillar of the company was Jan
Hoeufft, whose influence in financial and official circles in
Paris and connections in Amsterdam enabled him to draw in
capital from both those centers.[74]

In England efforts of Dutchmen to set up industries of their
own were brusquely extinguished by the unsleeping jealousy
of " true-born " Englishmen. That was the lot of Pieter Semeyn
who set up a furnace and forge in Wales for the manufacture
of ordnance which he exported to the Netherlands; [75] and the
lot of Paul Tymmerman, denizened but an alien still—at least to
his London competitors—when he attempted to operate a
sugar-refinery in that city. In the latter case it is noteworthy
that the London sugar-bakers alleged " that this Tymmerman
hath combined with divers strangers beyond Seas, and hath
their so greate a Stock of money, as if he should be suffered
to use this Art, either within or neere the Cittie, it would
sucke out the hart and sweete of this busines from the Englishe." [76]

In Scotland and Ireland there were industrial tentatives
linked with Holland. Thus we find " that weill accomplished
gentleman," Sir Philiberto Vernatti, of Dutch origin despite
his name, " hath perfytted that worke of making of glasse
in this kingdome " (Scotland), with eleven skilled glassblowers
whom he had induced to leave the service of their English
employer, Sir Robert Mansfield.[77] Clothmaking was essayed
in Edinburgh by William Dickson, once of Delft, with craftsmen imported from Holland, and Amsterdam capital was interested in the manufacture of cloth at Limerick and Dublin.[78]

[74] Édouard, Comte de Dienne, *Histoire du Desséchement des Lacs et Marais
en France avant 1789, passim;* Mathorez, *Les Étrangers en France,* II, 207,
233 ff.   On Hoeufft, see above, pp. 30, 105-106.
[75] *Acts of the Privy Council of England, 1613-1614,* ed. H. C. Maxwell-Lyte
(London, 1921), pp. 427, 446, May 7 and 23, 1614; *ibid., 1616-1617* (London,
1927), p. 47, Oct. 18, 1616.
[76] Public Record Office, State Papers, domestic, 14/87, no. 74. Newsletter by
Edward Sherburn, London, June 29, 1616.
[77] *Register of the Privy Council of Scotland, 1633-1635,* ed. P. H. Brown
(series 2, vol. V, Edinburgh, 1904), pp. 513, 518.
[78] *Extracts from the Records of the Burgh of Edinburgh,* eds. J. D. Marwick
and Marguerite Wood (Scottish Burghs Record Society, 6 vols., Edinburgh
1869-1892), II, 178, 198-202. E. Lipson, *The Economic History of England,*
III, 202; Gemeente Oud-Archief, Not. Arch. 3430, Notaris Cornelis van
Poelensurgh, Contracts of April-May, 1664 between Daniel Wijbrants and

We hear also of an oil-pressing mill set up in Limerick by a Scot resident in Amsterdam.[79]

Burghers of Amsterdam and other Netherlands towns were extensively interested in drainage undertakings in England, notably in those directed by the Zeelander, Cornelis Vermuyden, in York, Lincoln, and in the Great Level of the Fens. In 1628 a single Dutch investor was said to have put £13,000 into the draining of the Isle of Axholme.[80] In 1630 Vermuyden petitioned for the denization of eighteen of his associates in the draining of Hatfield Chace, of whom a majority were of Amsterdam.[81] One of the principal undertakers in this, as also in the Earl of Bedford's company for reclaiming the Great Fen, was that same " weill accomplished gentleman," Vernatti, whose glass-making enterprise in Scotland has just been mentioned. He too petitioned for the denization of " some of his frendes gentlemen of good Estates, yet aliens borne," whom he had induced to invest in the Fens project. First on his list of fourteen names is that of the veteran Amsterdam *rentier,* Reynier Pauw, and nearly all—possibly all—were of that city.[82]

In London there was far more of Dutch capitalism in action in the early Stuart period than in the enterprises we have been considering. That Dutch funds to vaguely large amounts were on loan in London in these years was often referred to

two other merchants of Amsterdam, with eight clothworkers of Leiden, who are to go to Dublin for a period of two years, to be employed in clothmaking.

[79] *Ibid.,* Not. Arch. 4601, Notaris Joannes Backer, Aug. 16, 1697; *ibid.,* 4616, the same notary, June 7, 1700. Both entries are of contracts made by Robert Pease, merchant of Amsterdam, the first with certain millwrights of Zaandam, who were to construct the mill at Limerick; the second with an oil-presser who was to operate it.

[80] *Calendar of State Papers, domestic series, 1628-1629,* ed. John Bruce (London, 1859), p. 262.

[81] Public Record Office, State Papers, domestic, 16/168, no. 3, June 1, 1630. For information about persons named in this petition, and in Vernatti's petition (see following note), I am indebted to Mr. Simon Hart, archivist in the Oud-Archief of Amsterdam. Of Dutch participation in these drainage projects there is much evidence in the *Calendar of State Papers, domestic series* for the years 1628-1635. On Vermuyden: J. Korthals Altes, *Sir Cornelius Vermuyden* (London, 1925), especially Chap. V.

[82] Public Record Office, State Papers, domestic, 16/257, no. 23, It was doubtless because of Amsterdam's interest in this enterprise that we find an account and diagram of it in *L'Atlas de Gerard Mercator et d'Hondius* (Amsterdam, 1633), I, pp. 140-141.

as a matter of common knowledge. After the Cockayne fiasco Dutch money assisted the Merchant Adventurers to buy back their charter from the king in 1617.[83] The arrest and trial in Star Chamber in 1618-1619 of eighteen prominent merchant strangers—most of them southern Netherlanders by birth or extraction, having family and business ties with Holland, and popularly referred to as ' Dutch '—on the charge of having exported coin to the fantastic sum of £7,000,000 may have been a blundering effort to stop the flow of interest payments to Holland, though speculative movements of the monetary metals, coined or uncoined, were, as we have seen, common in this century.[84] After unpublicized negotiations the cases were dropped and the merchants released with a round of fines, but the episode would seem to have administered a check to Dutch lending which may have been a factor in the financial crisis of 1621.[85] If so, recovery was prompt, for in 1624 a bill to reduce the legal interest maximum from 10 to 8 per cent, evoked the argument that it would cause the Dutch to call home their money.[86] In 1638 Lewes Roberts made a passing reference to Amsterdam capital in England: " Of late daies England, and other neighbouring Countries are found to have their estate going at interest according to the custome of the place, which is 8 per cent. whereas in their owne Countries 4. or 5. per cent. is as much as the same will yeeld them." [87] Thomas Violet, a goldsmith and an experienced hand in the international trade in bullion, who had left his native Antwerp to settle in London, estimated the foreign capital (which must have been in greater part Dutch) at use in England under the first Stuart kings, as in the neighborhood of £3,000,000.[88] Sir William Monson's extravagant invective

[83] Lipson, III, 212.

[84] For this episode see especially, *The Letters of John Chamberlain*, ed. N. E. McClure (2 vols., Philadelphia, 1939), II, 245, 267, 275 ff., 284. Among the arrested merchants were Philip Burlamachi, the two Courteens, Sir Peter van Lore, and others having business or family associations in the Netherlands.

[85] " Some were of opinion the withdrawing of the Dutch Merchants was the Cause of this sudden Damp." *Commons Debates, 1621*, eds. Notestein, Relf, and Simpson, V, 492, debate on scarcity of coin, Feb. 26, 1621.

[86] Lipson, III, 213.

[87] *The Merchants Mappe of Commerce* (1638), part ii, p. 111.

[88] *Letter to the Lord Chancellor* [1661?] p. 10. This is one of a number

may be quoted as an example of what some Englishmen chose
to believe of the intrusions of Dutch capitalism:

What trades and artifices of all kinds do they set up, to the ruin of
many a poor Englishman that has lived an apprentice and bondman
seven years to attain his art and occupation? What trades are there in
which they have not stocks going, or scriveners with money to lend?
What land is to be sold, or mortgage to be had, that they have not the
first refusal of? What marriages of man or woman falls amongst them
that they will enrich the English with so long as any of their country
or tribe is found amongst them? What maritime town, or other of
account within twenty miles of the sea, opposite to Holland, that is
not stuffed or filled with their people, to the impoverishing of the inhabitants and dwellers? What masses of money and gold have they,
against the laws of the realm, transported out of it as truth has made
it plain? [89]

Whatever the hard facts underlying this comprehensive in-
dignation, the seizure of merchants' monies in the Mint by
Charles I in 1640, and signs of approaching civil war, caused
foreign capital to take flight. Sir Thomas Roe was uncertain
whether this should be regarded as making for weal or woe,
and posed the problem to the House of Commons —

Whether it were profitable to a kingdom or not, that the stranger
for many years had a great stock, here at interest, and still hath some;
I confess it hath supplied the necessities of merchants, and helped to
drive trade. But my query is this, suppose the first principal were truly
brought in by the stranger, yet doubling every ten years; what becomes
of the increase? Have they not lived by our trade, and the merchant-
adventurers, and soaked the kingdom of as many times principal, as
they have practised this usury many times ten years, and in the end
drawn or carried all away? [90]

During the Interregnum the movement of capital seems to
have been from England to Holland, a fact which may have
helped to make insoluble the fiscal difficulties of Interregnum
governments.[91] At the Restoration Clarendon was eager to

of pamphlets by Violet in the library of the British Museum catalogued as
" Tracts relating to the Coinage " (714 h 12). One can entertain no illusions
about Violet's reliability in general, but this was a matter he was personally
concerned in, since he himself had been convicted of exporting coin in the
thirties.

[89] *The Naval Tracts of Sir William Monson,* ed. M. Oppenheim, V, 304.
[90] *Harleian Miscellany,* IV, 457-458, " Sir Thomas Roe's Speech in Parliament . . . "
[91] The apparent stability of the Protectorate shortly before its end would

lure Dutch investment capital back to England,[92] and there are indications that it came willingly. In 1668 Sir William Temple from the Hague advised reducing the interest paid by Charles II to English bankers from 10 to 8 per cent, saying he had reason to believe " a very great Trade is driven with them from Holland by Dutch Merchants, who turn their Mony through their Hands, encouraged by the great Interest they gaine there in lieu of so small here. . . ." [93] The following year the advisability of reducing the rate of interest was debated by a group of London merchants before a committee of the House of Lords, and the inevitable question was raised, of the effect of such action in discouraging Dutch capital. The proponents of reduction claimed that there was comparatively little Dutch money in London, not more than about £10,000, but their opponents declared that much of the money being used in trade and the rebuilding of London was of Dutch provenance, and that four London merchants, whom they named, had about £400,000 of Dutch money in their hands, which they lent out to merchants at 5, 6, or 7 per cent.[94]

After the Revolution of 1688 England became the preferred field for investment of Amsterdam capital. Though the owners of this capital were wary of subscription to the capital of the Bank of England at its foundation, perhaps from distrust of its close connection with government finance, yet during the vicissitudes of the years 1695-1697, Amsterdam money came to the rescue of the bank by taking over its protested bills, a service for which it charged no less than 10 per cent.[95]

seem to have attracted some Dutch capital. (Samuel Lambe, *Seasonable Observations*, p. 9.)

[92] " I must tell you, the making of this peace (if wee can hansomely bringe it to passe upon the old foote, which Crumwell went upon . . .) will have an excellent influence heere . . . this deadnesse of trade would be a little releived, and probably the Duch would agayne send ther mony hither for the benefitt of interest, and the dearth of mony heare, will be shortly to notorious . . . " Lister, *Life and Administration of Edward, first Earl of Clarendon*, III, 168, To Sir George Downing, Aug. 16, 1661.

[93] *Letters written by Sir William Temple*, II, 53-54, To the Lord Keeper, Nov. 2 (o.s.), 1668. See also, Josiah Child, *Brief Observations concerning Trade and Interest of Money* (1668), pp. 9-10.

[94] House of Lords MSS., Westminster, Minutes of a committee on the decay of trade, Oct. 28, 1669.

[95] Sir John Harold Clapham, *The Bank of England, a History* (2 vols.,

In the first quarter of the eighteenth century there was " a rush of Dutch investors " to buy stock in the bank, while in company financing, public loans, and speculative trading in stocks, Dutch money was active in London.[96] In 1711 Charles Davenant declared:

> The Dutch, more especially for these eight or nine years last past, have been deeply concerned in all the funds in their own, and in the hands of English and French merchants residing here, and of the Jews; they are known to have considerable sums in the annuities, lotteries, East India bonds, stocks of the companies, and all the loans that are in course of payment and the produce of such effects lodged here must be returned to them either in bullion, bills of exchange, or commodities, which will be a constant drain to England, and a weight against us in the balance of trade, so long as the funds continue.[97]

Although the States of Holland in 1700 forbade their subjects to lend money to foreign powers or participate in foreign companies, the subjects responded with extensive disobedience, investing in England in the South Sea Company and the British Fishery, and in France in the Mississippi Bubble.[98] An example of disobedience was set by one of the burgomasters of Amsterdam, Jeronimus de Haze di Giorgio, who put about two-thirds of his great fortune in English securities: f. 1,083,-880 in stock and annuities of the Bank of England, and f. 1,142,300 in stock of the South Sea Company—this latter much shrunken in value by the time of his death in 1725.[99]

Cambridge [Eng.], 1945), I, 28-29. At the same time the States of Holland lent the bank £300,000 (*ibid.*).

[96] On the " rush " of Dutch investment capital in the first quarter of the eighteenth century to buy stock in the bank: *ibid.*, I, 278, 282. By 1751 there were 105 Dutch shareholders—individuals, companies, and institutions—out of a total of 495 holding stock to the amount of £4,000 or more, and thereby eligible to the governorship. (*Ibid.*, I, 284.) On the role of Dutch capital in England from the Revolution through the third quarter of the eighteenth century: G. W. Kernkamp, "Amsterdamsche Patriciërs," *Vragen des Tijds,* XXXII, 38-39.

[97] *Works,* ed. Whitworth, V, 437. For similar expressions of anxiety over the extent of Dutch investment in England, see *Calendar of State Papers, domestic series, 1700-1702,* ed. Edward Bateson (London, 1937), pp. 607-608; Sir Francis Brewster, *New Essays on Trade* (London, 1702), p. 30.

[98] Kernkamp, " Amsterdamsche Patriciërs," *Vragen des Tijds,* XXXII, 38-39; Johannes A. Alting Boesken, *Over Geldleeningen hier te Lande door Vreemde Mogendheden aangegaan* (Utrecht, 1864), p. 22. For a spiteful explanation of the causes of this extensive investment in English securities, see *Mémoires de Saint-Simon,* ed. A. de Boislisle (43 vols., Paris, 1879-1930), XXIX, 268 ff.

[99] Kernkamp, *Vragen des Tijds,* XXXII, 38.

Hamburg was not only Amsterdam's rival for the commerce of northern Europe, but was also an outpost or subsidiary of Amsterdam's trade and capitalism. The number of burghers of Netherlands birth or extraction in Hamburg was large—so large that English policy sometimes assumed that Hamburgers were Hollanders disguised as neutrals. " That there are above 400 Netherlands Merchants settled with their families in the Citty of Hamburgh, who are all of the obedience of the States Generall . . . That most of the Burgers of that Citty who are Marchants, are by extraction of those Netherlands, driven thence in the time of Duke d'Alva and maintayne their relations still." [100] Many successful Amsterdam merchants carried on some part of their business in the Hanseatic city, among them Louis de Geer, Johan Deutz, and the Marcelises and Van der Straten. During the war with Spain a substantial part of Dutch trade with countries under Spanish sovereignty was transacted through Hamburg intermediaries, and in the English wars Dutch ships easily transformed themselves into Hamburg ships. On the other hand, when the republic was at peace, Dutch ships carried much of Hamburg's trade. In 1665 almost half of all Hamburg merchants engaged in foreign trade had a trade or commission business with Holland.[101] The exchange business carried on between these two commercial cities was greater than their trade in commodities.[102] Passenger, freight, and postal services which connected them were regular and frequent, employing a large number of vessels throughout this century. Part of the capital which founded the bank of Hamburg in 1619 was subscribed from Amsterdam, and certain ' Danish ' trading companies were established by combined Amsterdam and Hamburg capital.[103]

A few grandiose projects which were not realized or had no long life illustrate the bold, pushful spirit of Amsterdam

[100] Public Record Office, State Papers, foreign, Hamburg 8, ff. 208-209, " Paper of Mr. Skinner concerning the proposition of the Agent of Hamburg " (1652).

[101] Ernest Baasch, "Hamburg and Holland im 17. und 18. Jahrhundert," *Hansische Geschichtsblätter*, (1910), XVI, 55-56.

[102] Le Moine de l'Espine, *Le Négoce d'Amsterdam* (1694), pp. 132-133.

[103] On the relation between Amsterdam capital and the bank of Hamburg: H. Sieveking, " Die Hamburger Bank," *History of the Principal Public Banks*, p. 127. On the collaboration of Amsterdam capital with Hamburg capital in the Danish companies, see below, pp. 133, 135.

capitalism: the attempt made in 1608, and again ten years later, to set up a monopoly for the export of Russian grain; [104] similar efforts to obtain exclusive control of the trans-Russian trade in Persian silks; [105] the scheme for compulsory insurance of merchant shipping, the promoters of which gracefully allocated to themselves as part compensation a monopoly of the trade with Barbary and Italy; [106] that towering consortium of Amsterdam capitalists formed by Trip and De Geer in 1634 with a capital of f. 2,400,000 to handle Swedish copper exports;[107] the contract, previously referred to, which four Amsterdammers concluded with the Swedish regents in 1663 for a monopoly of exporting iron cannon to Amsterdam; [108] efforts of the Royal Tar Company of Sweden, a creation of Louis and Hendrick Trip, to control prices of pitch and tar; [109] an alleged project of 1658 for farming the tolls of the Sound in case Sweden should succeed Denmark in sovereignty over that waterway; [110] negotiations, presumably by the directors of the Levant trade, to lease a port on the island of Elba to be used as staple for the Mediterranean trade; [111] an alleged proposal to handle the entire foreign trade of Poland or,

---

[104] S. van Brakel, *De Hollandsche Handelscompagniën der Zeventiende Eeuw,* pp. 23-24; Scheltema, I, 61 ff. 127, 140-141; Aitzema, II, 801 ff.; Elias, "Contract tot Oprichting van een Zweedsch Factorie-comptoir," *Bijdragen en Mededeelingen,* XXIV, 360 ff.; D. S. van Zuiden, "Nieuwe Bijdrage tot de Kennis van de Hollandsch-Russische Relaties," *Economisch-historisch Jaarboek* (1916), II, 270 ff.

[105] M. N. Pokrovskii, *History of Russia from the Earliest Times to the Rise of Commercial Capitalism,* translated and edited by J. D. Clarkson and M. R. M. Griffiths (New York, *c.* 1931), p. 267, Scheltema, I, 104, 113, 146, 178, 335-336; Boris Raptschinsky, "Bescheiden betreffende het Gezantschap van Koenraad van Klenck naar Moscovie in 1675-1676," *Bijdragen en Mededeelingen* (1938), LIX, 87 ff., 121.

[106] P. J. Blok, "Het Plan tot Oprichting eener Compagnie van Assurantie," *Bijdragen voor Vaderlandsche Geschiedenis en Oudheidkunde* (1900), series 4, vol. I, 1 ff.; and edited by the same, "Koopmansadviezen aangaande het Plan tot Oprichting eener Compagnie van Assurantie 1629-1635," *Bijdragen en Mededeelingen* (1900), XXI, 1 ff.; Aitzema, II, 708 ff., 726 ff.

[107] J. G. van Dillen, "Amsterdamsche Notarieele Acten betreffende den Koperhandel," *Bijdragen en Mededeelingen* (1937), LVIII, 220 ff., 263 ff.

[108] Elias, "Contract," *Bijdragen,* XXIV, pp. 356 ff., 391 ff.

[109] Rijks Archief, Staten Generaal, Lias Zweden 6542, C. C. Rumpf to the States General, Sept. 4, 1677. See also below, p. 131.

[110] *State Papers of John Thurloe,* ed. T. Birch, VII, 442.

[111] *Correspondance Administrative sous le règne de Louis XIV,* ed. Depping, III, 349-350.

failing that, to obtain exclusive right to import cloth into that kingdom; [112] the project, already alluded to, of a group of Amsterdam merchants to equip, arm, provision, and pay the imperial army; [113] a transportation business set up by two members of the Deutz family in 1682 to handle shipments of goods from Amsterdam to destinations elsewhere in the United Provinces, the Baltic, Germany, Italy, and Smyrna, and take on return cargoes; [114] and a project by certain Amsterdam and Leiden merchants to set up under their own direction a manufacture of camlets at Ankara in Turkey.[115]

[112] Public Record Office, State Papers, foreign, Poland 12, Francis Sanderson, Danzig, to Joseph Williamson, Dec. 27, 1670.

[113] Above, p. 40.

[114] Elias, *De Vroedschap van Amsterdam*, II, 634-635.

[115] Gemeente Oud-Archief, Arch. Burg., Portefeuille Handel 3, Information from Smyrna, dated April 7, 1698.

CHAPTER VII

CHARACTERISTICS OF AMSTERDAM CAPITALISM

The cosmopolitan spirit and geographical dispersion of certain merchant families whose business headquarters were in Amsterdam, interestingly foreshadowed the international histories of later capitalist families. The international capitalist from his earliest to his latest appearance has generally been, where business was concerned, a Man without a Country, and the seventeenth-century Amsterdammer, though by no means a man without a city, was strikingly uninhibited by abstract considerations of patriotism or by theories of economic nationalism. One can understand why this was so. In the historic past the loyalty of Netherlanders had centered more strongly in province or town than in such widespread and remote-seeming sovereignties as Burgundy, the Empire, or ' the Spains '; and in the seventeenth century these local loyalties were still stronger than any as yet commanded by the loose confederation of the United Provinces. But in this century of warring religious convictions, many successful merchant dynasties of Amsterdam had, in coming there, sacrificed their allegiances to native towns and provinces on the altar of conscience. Their first loyalty was to creed. For economic nationalism the country was too small and too poor in natural resources. Though complaints were occasionally voiced that Hollanders were too greedy for riches to put their money into trade, industry, or land, and therefore invested their funds in foreign countries,[1] it is probable that trade, industry and agriculture got all the capital they could use with prospect of profit.

The extraordinarily dense population of Holland, which amazed foreign visitors, lived by trade and activities stemming from trade, and could not long forego intercourse with any trading country, whether friend or foe. Trade with the enemy must contribute to war with the enemy. Why make

---

[1] Etienne Laspeyres, *Geschichte der Volkswirthschaftlichen Anschauungen der Niederländer und ihrer Litteratur zur Zeit der Republik* (Leipzig, 1863), p. 254.

a present of that trade to Hamburg or England? The great profits to be derived from contraband trade lent cogency to this argument. During the war with Spain Amsterdam merchants had not only traded with the enemy—that was common enough—but had invested in Dunkirk privateers which preyed on Dutch shipping.[2] Laurens de Geer, Swedish subject yet burgher of Amsterdam, was suspected of selling munitions to England during the first Anglo-Dutch war.[3] In 1659, a year when both the Dutch navy and the merchant fleet were in great need of tar, the brothers Trip declined to sell their holdings of that indispensable commodity except at monopoly prices, and in the meantime were shipping out consignments of tar, some of which may have reached the enemy.[4] As we have seen, the contract to exploit the republic's dependence on Swedish munitions was signed on the eve of the second war with England.[5] Amsterdam did not refrain from providing cordage and sailcloth for the English navy during the English wars.[6] The terrible famine which struck at defeated France in 1709, was relieved by a fleet of Dutch grain-carriers from the Baltic, in which some principal merchants of Amsterdam were said to be interested.[7] Financing the enemy was easier than trade with the enemy, movements of credit and even of coin being more difficult to trace than movements of ships. Credits necessary to keep the French armies on foot were remitted from Amsterdam by exchange on Geneva, thence to Lyon, and so to Paris.[8] Specie consignments were made to

---

[2] Sayous, "Die grossen Händler und Kapitalisten in Amsterdam," *Weltwirtschaftliches Archiv*, XLVII, 126; Elias: *De Vroedschap van Amsterdam*, I, xlvi; Van Dillen, "Amsterdam in Bredero's Tijd," *De Gids*, XCIX, part ii, p. 316

[3] Elias, *Bijdragen*, XXIV, 372.

[4] Gemeente Oud-Archief, Missiven van de Raad, no. 3, Aan de Gedeputeerden, Oct. 3, 1659.

[5] Elias, *Bijdragen*, XXIV, 383 ff.

[6] *Recueil des Instructions données aux Ambassadeurs et Ministres de France depuis les Traités de Westphalie jusqu'à la Révolution Française*, nos. xxiv-xxv, *Angleterre*, ed. J. J. Jusserand (2 vols., Paris, 1929), II, 205. On the sale of munitions to France, see above, p. 40.

[7] Wijnand Bunk, *Staathuishoudkundige Geschiedenis van den Amsterdamschen Graanhandel*, p. 83.

[8] André-E. Sayous, "Le Financier Jean-Henri Huguetan à Amsterdam et à Genève," *Bulletin de la Société d'Histoire et d'Archéologie de Genève* (1937), VI, 255 ff.; and by the same, "La Crise Financière de 1709 à Lyon et à Genève," *ibid.*, VI, 354 ff.

bankers in the Spanish Netherlands, thence to find their way into the towns recently annexed by France.[9]

Amsterdam was incurably cooperative towards foreign companies, including those founded to supplant the Dutch in important branches of their trade. In successive French attempts to open a trade to the East Indies, Dutchmen had some part, and Amsterdam was somewhere in the background. Thus in the East India Company projected by Gérard de Roy, who had made a voyage or voyages to the East, presumably in one of the expeditions sent out from Amsterdam by the *vóórcompagniën*, moving spirits were Balthasar de Moucheron of Middelburg, Pieter Lintgens, a Hollander, and Isaac Le Maire, ex-Antwerpenaar settled in Amsterdam, who had subscribed f. 60,000 to the stock of the United East India Company of 1602, but had later been expelled from that company. We have met him before as speculator in the company's actions.[10] In the grand but still-born project of Richelieu for a general company for trade and colonization, we find the Hollander Nicolas Witte.[11] A French plan to initiate trade with China was set on foot in 1660. The principal ship of the contemplated flotilla, the *St. Louis,* was built and equipped in Amsterdam and, as De Witt wrote: "Apparently the first move in this matter came from here, and for the most part it was inhabitants of Holland who were concerned in it, the shipmaster and almost all of the principal officers of this ship being Hollanders."[12] Colbert's East India Company, founded in 1664, attracted a number of secessionists from the Dutch company, chief among them François Caron, who had occupied a position of trust in the service of the United East India Company in Japan, and now organized and shared in the direction of the first French expedition to the Indies.[13] This fleet was in

[9] *Correspondance des Contrôleurs Généraux des Finances,* ed. De Boislisle, II, 400-401.

[10] Above, p. 77; Van Dillen, "Isaac Le Maire," *Revue,* X, 10 ff.; Gustave Fagniez, "Le Commerce Extérieur de la France sous Henri IV, 1589-1610," *Revue Historique* (1881), XVI, 16-17.

[11] *Lettres, Instruction Diplomatiques et Papiers d'État du Cardinal de Richelieu,* ed. Avenel, VIII, 195.

[12] *Brieven . . . Johan de Witt,* I, 330-331, To Van Beuningen, Dec. 2, 1660. (Translation)

[13] Bodleian Library, Clarendon MS. 107, ff. 109 b, 138, translations of letters dated Feb. 29 and March 28, 1664, from Boreel, Dutch ambassador

part outfitted in the Netherlands, and the Amsterdam house of Coymans acted as agent for the French company.[14]

When the first joint-stock of the English East India Company was afoot in 1614, we find an Amsterdammer, Pieter Hoote, knocking at the door. He had lived some thirteen years in the Indies in the service of the Dutch company, and now agreed to adventure £4,000 in the English company's stock, besides £400 for his freedom and the broke.[15]

The first Danish East India Company, erected in 1616, was launched by two Hollanders, Jan de Willem and Herman Rosenkrantz. Both were domiciled in Copenhagen, but De Willem had a brother in Amsterdam, like himself immersed in Danish affairs.[16] In 1621 the ubiquitous Isaac Le Maire was contemplating entering this company with his Amsterdam associates.[17] The first expedition was ably and vigorously directed by Marcelis de Boshauer who, in the employ of the Dutch company had shown greater enterprise in the penetration of Ceylon than the directors were prepared to approve. Though De Boshauer died on this voyage, the company seized Tranquebar, and thereafter from time to time sent out small trading ventures to the East, usually with Dutch masters, Dutch pilots, and some Dutch and Hamburg capital engaged.[18] By the middle of the century the company was deeply in debt and had ceased to trade, but in 1670 it was reorganized, again with Dutch participation. This time direction was in the hands of Ernst and Jan van Hoogenhoeck, the former of whom had long served the Dutch company in Japan. The three shipmasters who went out with the first expedition in 1674 had also been employed by the United East India Company, and had taken service with the Danish organization because the

in Paris, to the States General; *Correspondance Administrative sous le régne de Louis XIV*, ed. Depping, III, 438, Colbert to Pomponne, May 3, 1669; Cole, *Colbert and a Century of French Mercantilism*, I, 506 ff.; Paul Kaeppelin, *Les Origines de l'Inde français . . . (1664-1719)*, pp. 89 ff.

[14] Kaeppelin, p. 8; S. Elzinga, *Het Voorspel van den Oorlog van 1672*, p. 200.

[15] *Calendar of State Papers, colonial series, East Indies, China and Japan, 1513-1616*, ed. W. Noel Sainsbury (London, 1862), pp. 311, 324, 328-329.

[16] Catharina Ligtenberg, *Willem Usselinx* (Utrecht, 1914), p. 85.

[17] G. W. Kernkamp, "Memoriën van Ridder Theodorus Rodenburg," *Bijdragen en Mededeelingen* (1902), XXIII, 246-247.

[18] F. Dekker, *Voortrekkers van Oud-Nederland uit Nederlands Geschiedenis buiten de Grenzen* (Den Haag, 1938), pp. 156-157.

latter permitted them to do some trading for themselves, which was strictly prohibited by the Dutch company. Initial success was followed by disaster in 1677 when a large and richly laden ship, the *Oldenburgh,* at the beginning of her voyage to India was lost with all save four of her complement of about 200 men, among them Jan van Hoogenhoeck, several members of his family, and many Hollanders who were going out as assistants, bookkeepers, and merchants in the service of the Danish company.[19]

Netherlanders who were not of Amsterdam, but whose knowledge of the East India trade was probably picked up in that city, are found laying plans for an East Indian trade from Tuscany in 1608, from Scotland in 1622, and from Brandenburg in 1681.[20]

West India (or Guinea or African) companies launched in several countries had a leaven of Dutch enterprise, and a suspicion, or more than that, of Dutch capital. Thus the Danish West India Company organized by Jan de Willem and his Amsterdam friends in 1625, was prepared to send out its first expedition without any participation by Danish capital.[21] A Swedish African Company was chartered in 1649 by the enterprise of Louis de Geer who, with the cooperation of Amsterdam, found five-sixths of the capital. Direction of the company was placed in the hands of Laurens de Geer, who managed his father's business interests in Amsterdam. International competition for the lion's share of the slave trade was intensified by the versatility of one Hendrik Caerloff, a

[19] Rijks Archief, Staten Generaal, Lias Denemarken, 5920, From Le Maire, Copenhagen, July 7, 1674; *ibid.,* Lias Denemarken 5921, from the same, Feb. 16, 1677.

[20] For the attempt made in 1608 by an anonymous writer, possibly a Netherlander living in Livorno, to interest the Grand Duke of Tuscany in the East Indian trade, see Sebastiano Crinò, "Samenwerking tusschen de Republiek der Geunieerde Gewesten en het Groothertogdom Toscane, op het Gebied van den Overzeeschen Handel," *Mededeelingen van het Neder-landsch Historisch Instituut te Rome,* 2d ser., (1933), III, 115 ff. Lucas Corsellis, a Netherlander from the southern provinces who settled in London, seems to have projected a Scottish India Co. in 1622. *(Calendar of State Papers, domestic series, 1619-1623,* p. 434.) On a Brandenburg expedition to the East Indies fitted out by the brothers Raulé (see below, p. 135.), with assistance from other Zeelanders: Rijks Archief, Resolutiën Staten Generaal, CXXII, f. 448, June 7, 1681.

[21] Kernkamp, "Memoriën van Ridder Theodorus Rodenburg," *Bijdragen,* XXIII, 212-213; Ligtenberg, p. 95.

native of Rostock, it is believed, who from serving the Dutch West India Company as *commies-fiscaal* in Guinea, was won over to the Swedish company by Laurens de Geer. When the De Geer heirs lost control of the company to Swedish stockholders in 1657, Caerloff organized in Amsterdam and with the cooperation of several highly-placed citizens, an African Company of Glückstadt, nominally Danish, for which two obliging Hamburgers supplied a façade. Its trading, however, was managed by Caerloff and other former agents of the Dutch company. An intercompany war for possession of forts and lodges on the slave coast ensued, in which Negro tribes were encouraged to participate, and the recently founded Royal African Company of England found good fishing in troubled waters. Caerloff, it is interesting to note, changed allegiance again, and is last heard of in the service of the French West India Company.[22] We need not follow the territorial claims of the companies into the realm of diplomacy, where they were eventually settled.

A Brandenburg African Company had been originally projected by Aernoult Gijsels van Lier, a native of Gelders, who had been governor of Amboyna under the Dutch company. Nothing came of this tentative, but in 1680 the subject was resumed by Benjamin Raulé of a Flemish family settled in Middelburg, where this particular scion became a prosperous merchant and official of the city, with an account in the bank of Amsterdam. In 1675 he is found sending out privateers under the flag of Brandenburg to capture Dutch ships carrying Swedish trade. Five years later he had risen to be economic adviser and minister of marine to the Elector of Brandenburg, and promoter of a company to open trade with Guinea and Angola. This company was ostensibly of Königsberg, but capital, ships, shipmasters and factors were of Zeeland and Holland.[23]

[22] Breedvelt-Van Veen, *Louis de Geer*, pp. 146 ff.; Johan E. Elias, "De Tweede Engelsche Oorlog als het Keerpunt in onze Betrekkingen met Engeland," *Verhandelingen der Koninklijke Akademie van Wetenschappen te Amsterdam, Afdeeling Letterkunde* (1930), new ser., XXIX, no. 5, pp. 26 ff.; N. de Roever, "Twee Concurrenten van de eerste West-Indische Compagnie," *Oud-Holland* (1889), VII, 199 ff.; J. Kretzschmar, "Schwedische Handelskompanien," *Hansische Geschichtsblätter*, XVII, 237 ff.; Mims, *Colbert's West India Policy*, pp. 117-118, 165 ff., 172, 285; Cole, II, 9, 20-21.

[23] Rudolf Häpke, "Benjamin Raulé und seine Handlungsbücher," *Economisch-*

The spacious and idealistic plans of Willem Usselincx, one of the many ex-Antwerpenaars resident in Amsterdam, for the colonization of the New World as a new world, found no sympathetic hearing in realistic Amsterdam, and the West India Company was modelled fairly closely after the East India Company. Disillusioned, Usselincx went off to Sweden, where he obtained a charter for his Söderkompanie, but the project got no further. It remained for two practical Amsterdammers, Samuel Blommaert and Peter Minuit, to screen out the · idealism and make a business proposition of the Söderkompanie. The former was a merchant who by trade or investment had become interested in Sweden, and had proffered economic advice to Chancellor Oxenstierna. Minuit, a native of Wesel long resident in Amsterdam, had served the West India Company as governor of New Amsterdam. Together they entered Usselincx's hitherto inactive company, Minuit bringing with him several of his fellow officials of the West India Company. In all, Amsterdam supplied one-half of the capital of f. 24,000 which launched the colony of New Sweden. The brief initial success of this enterprise, followed by the snuffing out of the infant Swedish settlement on the Delaware river by the Dutch company, need not be retold here.[24]

Although several of the projects we have been reviewing were matters of common knowledge in Amsterdam, little effort was made to bring offenders to book even when a legal monopoly was violated. In the tangled episode of the rivalry of Dutch-sponsored ' Danish ' and ' Swedish ' companies with the West India Company for primacy in the slave trade, the fact emerged that Isaac Coymans, a wealthy merchant of

historisch Jaarboek (1923), IX, 218 ff.; R. Schuck, Brandenburg-Preussens Kolonialpolitik unter dem Grossen Kurfürsten und seinen Nachfolgern (1647-1721) (2 vols., Leipzig, 1889), I, 235 ff., 240 ff., 251. This matter was frequently noticed in the States General in the years 1680-1682. (Rijks Archief, Resolutiën Staten Generaal, CXXI-CXXIV, passim.)

[24] Ligtenberg, passim; J. Franklin Jameson, "Willem Usselincx, Founder of the Dutch and Swedish West India Companies," Papers of the American Historical Association (New York, 1887), II, 1 ff., especially p. 184; "Brieven van Samuel Blommaert aan den Zweedschen Rijkskanselier Axel Oxenstierna, 1635-1641," in "Zweedsche Archivalia," ed. G. W. Kernkamp, Bijdragen en Mededeelingen (1908), XXIX, 67 ff.; Kretzschmar, Hansische Geschichtsblätter, XVII, 237 ff.

Amsterdam who had twice represented the West India Company in Africa, had been detected in correspondence of a treasonable nature with the 'Danish' company; had even incited it to stir up Negro tribes to attack the Dutch factories on the coast of Guinea. The revelation not unnaturally made a noise in the city, and Coymans was at first proceeded against with exemplary severity, but in the end he was let off rather easily.[25] As we have seen, De Witt condemned promotion by Amsterdammers of French plans to enter the Far Eastern trade, and the States General made the futile gesture of banning investment in foreign companies. In 1668 De Groot, Dutch ambassador at Stockholm, wrote his mind on this subject with reference to Swedish companies, "being convinced that all the misfortune which our countrymen encounter here and elsewhere, is set on foot and organized by Netherlanders who have settled here, and are the greatest stockholders and directors in the companies which are adjudged so injurious to the commerce of the inhabitants of our country."[26] But no genuine effort was made to check this expatriation of capital and enterprise. Had it been made, and made so effectively as to check the free outflow of capital to foreign countries, it must have resulted in an evasive exodus of that capital, and so in an earlier termination of the city's primacy as money market of Europe than actually occurred. On the contrary the States General showed a tender concern for the property rights and economic interests of its subjects and ex-subjects in foreign lands, and often interceded with the governments of those countries in their behalf.

Much of the eagerness to get into foreign East-Indian and African companies may be ascribed to resentment of those excluded from all but the meagerest share in the trade of three continents by the charters of the two India companies. Some of it sprang from impatience and frustration within the companies at the narrow conservatism, inertia, and dog-in-the-manger attitude of the directors.[27] The East India Com-

---

[25] H. Bontemantel, *De Regeeringe van Amsterdam soo in 't civiel als crimineel en militaire (1653-1672)*, ed. G. W. Kernkamp (2 vols., 's-Gravenhage, 1897, Werken uitg. door het Historisch Genootschap gevestigd te Utrecht, 3rd ser., nos. 7-8), I, ccii ff., 264 ff., II, 126, 377 ff.

[26] *Brieven . . . Johan de Witt,* II, 590-591, Sept. 5, 1668. (Translation)

[27] Isaac Le Maire was critical of the management of the East India Com-

pany's policy of scarcity, or 'keeping the market hungry,' was unquestionably a brake on expansion of the Eastern trade. It is noteworthy that certain owners of herring-busses of Rotterdam expressed a willingness to remove to Denmark provided they might be permitted to enter the Danish East India Company.[28] Usselincx declared in 1645 that if the East India Company's charter were renewed in its existing form, many experienced Dutch merchants would emigrate to places where they might be free to engage in trade to the Far East.[29] When, in the depths of the republic's misfortunes in 1672, English agents attempted to persuade the provinces of Holland and Zeeland to put themselves under the king of England's protection, certain " chief men of Rotterdam and Dort " were willing to negotiate " if they were but sure of a certain share in the trade of the [English] East India Company." [30]

It would be idle to speculate on the results to the republic, to Europe, and to the world, if the energy, ambition, and capital resources expended by Netherlanders in other countries of Europe had been directed towards overseas settlement. Voices were not lacking to urge a more statesmanlike and farsighted colonial policy on the States General than that pursued by the India companies. Jan Pietersz. Coen, distinguished governor-general of the East India Company's possessions, had stressed in a memorandum of 1623, the arguments of overpopulation and excess of investment capital.[31] The proposals

pany in 1609, but this was scarcely surprising as he had been forced out of it a few years earlier. (Van Dillen, " Isaac Le Maire," *Revue*, X, 123-124.) There were to be many pamphlet attacks on the board of directors *(bewindhebbers)*, a body over which the shareholders had no control, with allegations of corruption, incompetence, speculation, waste, and nepotism. (Laspeyres, pp. 68 ff.; Van Brakel, *De Hollandsche Handelscompagniën*, pp. 129 ff.) Pieter de la Court roundly denounced company trade in general on the grounds that lazy and unenterprising merchants were protected by the company's monopoly against competition, and that management of the companies was so extravagant that they could afford to carry on no trade which did not yield a high rate of profit. *(True Interest,* pp. 71 ff.)

[28] G. W. Kernkamp, " Memoriën van Ridder Theodorus Rodenburg," *Bijdragen* XXIII, 224.

[29] Ligtenberg, p. 229.

[30] Public Record Office, State Papers, foreign, Flanders 40, f. 213 v., J. Nipho, Bruges, to Joseph Williamson, July 19/29, 1672.

[31] G. W. Kernkamp, "Amsterdamsche Patriciërs," *Vragen des Tijds*, XXXII, 30.

of Johan Maurits of Nassau for the colonization of Brazil
and opening of the trade thither not only to Dutchmen but
to foreigners, met with obstruction from the West India
Company similar to that which Coen's ideas encountered from
the East India Company.[32] When Brazil had been lost to the
feeble Portuguese power, La Court pointed out that " by an
open Trade, and consequently well settled Colonies, we should
not only, with small Charge, have easily defended those vast
Lands of Brazil, Guiney, Angola, St. Thomas &c. against all
foreign Power, but . . . have been able to carry on a very great
Trade with our own Nation, without fear that any foreign
Potentate should seize our Ships, Goods, or Debts, to which
those Hollanders that trade only in Europe are continually
exposed." [33] He claimed that, contrary to received opinion,
Netherlanders made better colonists than any other nation.
" And those that doubt hereof, let them please to observe, that
the Hollanders . . . even under Foreign Princes, have made very
many new Colonies, namely in Lyfland, Prussia, Brandenburgh,
Pomerania, Denmark, Sleswick, France, England, Flanders, &c.
And moreover, have not only manured unfruitful unplanted
Lands, but also undertaken the chargeable and hazardous task
of draining of Fenlands." [34] Views such as these received
small attention in Amsterdam, where the great merchant
houses preferred an empire of trade, snug monopolies, and
the expectation of quick profits to the unpredictable, un-
collectible returns from colonization. In 1661, when peace
with Portugal and abandonment of Brazil were being dis-
cussed, the English resident, after mentioning the opposition of
Zeeland to peace, partly on the score of the interest of its inhabitants in Brazil, but even more because its privateers were
doing well in the matter of Portuguese prizes, analyzed the
attitude of Holland thus:

Holland on the other hand considers that it would be too costly a worke
to goe about the regaining Brazeile by force, especiallye considering
that the King of England is like to bee soe well enclyned towards
Portugall, and besides that if they had Brazeile, they knowe not how
to gett people to plant it, and therefore that it is better for them to
make Peace and content themselves with Trafficque thither, besides
the Holland East Indye Company have ever bin in an ill understanding

---

[32] Ligtenberg, p. 193.   [33] True Interest, p. 86.   [34] Ibid., p. 154.

with the Holland West Indy Companye, and doe not desire they should gett up again, yet on the other hand they would keepe off the Peace a while, at least in relation to the East Indyes, and to that effecte gave in a request yesterday to the States of Holland representing that they had bin at the expence of 85. Tunns of Gold, and desireing that such a time might bee sett for that Peace its takeing place in the East Indyes, as that they might not loose the benefitt of this years Equipage.[35]

There is no reason to suppose that a poll of merchant opinion in Amsterdam at this time would have favored more enlightened or more broadly national views.

As one reviews the unfolding capitalism of Amsterdam, it is evident that its strength lay in extension and intensification, not in experiment or innovation. The most familiar type of business organization in the city was the oldest of all such organizations, the family partnership or company. Business connections were quite commonly cemented and invested with relative permanence by intermarriages within the families concerned. Marriages of convenience among the patrician families of Amsterdam were not less common than among the English gentry or the French aristocracy. Great fortunes, it has been noted, were generally built up by continuous efforts of successive generations within families.[36] To this continuity the education of women in business made striking contribution. Most of the women who made names for themselves in business were widows carrying on their husbands' affairs until their sons should come of age, and not seldom continuing in partnership with them afterwards. Thus of ten women trading to the Mediterranean in 1646-1647, all but one were widows.[37] One should not think of them, however, as merely conserving and transmitting inherited wealth. Certain of them —the Widow Deutz, the Widow Thibaut, the Widow Rogge— displayed acumen and capacity in their affairs.

There was another aspect of the continuity of Dutch business houses which English and French observers stressed, and perhaps overstressed. Though capital went into land and in-

---

[35] Bodleian Library, Clarendon MS. 104, f. 136, Sir George Downing, from the Hague, to Clarendon, June 14/24, 1661.

[36] Kernkamp, "Amsterdamsche Patriciërs," *Vragen des Tijde*, XXXII, 35.

[37] Hermann Wätjen, *Die Niederländer im Mittelmeergebiet zur Zeit ihrer höchsten Machtstellung* [Abhandlungen zur Verkehrs- und Seegeschichte, no. 2, Berlin, 1909], p. 360.

dustry at home and abroad, as we have seen; went into *rentebrieven* and company stocks; went into the acquisition of public office and expense incidental thereto; into fine houses and luxurious living; it was surplus capital in excess of that needed for trade, shipping, and other forms of commercial investment. "The Dutch maister us in Trade," said Josiah Child. "Wee alwayes begin young men heere, there it holds from generation to generation." [38] And Jacques Savary wrote gloomily:

From the moment that a merchant in France has acquired great wealth in trade, his children, far from following him in this profession, on the contrary enter public office . . . whereas in Holland the children of merchants ordinarily follow the profession and the trade of their fathers, ally themselves with other merchant families, and give such considerable sums to their children when they marry that one of these will have greater wealth when he begins trading on his own, than the richest merchant of France will have when he stops trading to establish his family in other professions: therefore, since money is not withdrawn from trade, but continues in it constantly from father to son, and from family to family as a result of the alliances which merchants make with one another, individual Dutch merchants can more easily undertake the Northern and Muscovy trades than individual French merchants can undertake them.[39]

A very common form of business cooperation in seventeenth century Holland, common elsewhere in Europe and probably of mediaeval origin, was known as *rederij*. This was a highly flexible type of joint enterprise by which capitals large and small were combined for a purpose limited as to scope or as to time. A group of *reders* might join in building, buying, chartering, or freighting a ship, or might make a collective venture in a fishing or trading voyage. They might take shares, as we find them doing in the Zaan villages, in a mill, a train-cookery, a lighter, an anchor-smithy, a rope-walk, a lime-kiln, or a starch factory. An interesting joint enterprise of this nature was the construction and operation of the Zaandam *overtoom*, an ingenious mechanism by which ships were hauled over the bar separating the upper from the lower basin of the Zaan. There were sixty-four shares in this utility. Whether

---

[38] House of Lords MSS, Westminster, Minutes of a Committee on the decay of trade, Oct. 28, 1669.

[39] *Le Parfait négociant*, book ii, p. 112. (Translation)

these humble forms of combination were as common in Amsterdam as in the Zaan industries, cannot be answered with certainty. We hear of *rederij* in building and freighting ships, in whaling expeditions, and in the Norway timber trade, but not in the variety of small enterprises for which it was utilized in the Zaan villages.[40]

For the instruction of French merchants Savary described the various types of companies common in his time, concluding with the *sociétés anonymes* frequently formed by Dutch merchants and factors trading in France. These were not the limited liability companies to which the name *sociétés anonymes* was later to be applied, but secret and temporary combinations of buyers or sellers of some particular commodity or group of commodities in a particular market, with the object of influencing prices; in other words, merchant rings whose members ostensibly traded as individuals, but were actually in agreement on price strategy.[41] We have noticed that similar groups to control trading in certain commodities were formed in Amsterdam from time to time.[42] Though not peculiar to that city, they were probably more common in that greatest of markets than elsewhere in Europe.

There was indeed no institution nor any practice common in Amsterdam's business in this century—the trading in actions excepted—which had not been earlier known and used in the Italian cities, or Lyon, or Augsburg, or Antwerp: bourse, joint-stock company, cartel, banking and exchange, brokerage and insurance. Amsterdam gave these more precise formulation, greater flexibility and extension, and used them effectively over a wider field. Europe learned much from her, but her golden age was rather the climax of a period of transition than the beginning of a new economic era.

[40] Aris van Braam, *Bloei en Verval,* pp. 64 ff., S. Lootsma, *Historische Studiën over de Zaanstreek,* p. 218, note 2.

[41] *Le Parfait négociant,* book i, pp. 351 ff., 372 ff.

[42] Above, p. 75.

INDEX

Aachen, 35, 37.

Abbott, Wilbur Cortez, *see* Cromwell, Oliver.

Acts and Ordinances of the Interregnum, see Firth, C. H.

Acts of the Privy Council of England, 38 n., 121 n.

Adelaar, Cort, 115.

Africa, 137;
   trading companies, Brandenburg, Danish, English, Swedish, 134-135, *see also,* Guinea Company, West India companies;
   troops, 41.

Agio (premium) of bank money, 47, 79.

Ailly, A. E. d', ed., *Zeven Eeuwen Amsterdam,* 17 n., 20 n., 104 n., 105 n., 144, 145.

Aitzema, Lieuwe van, *Historie of Verhael van Saken van Staet en Oorlogh,* 91 n., 104 n., 105 n., 128 n.

Algiers, 54.

Alicante, 91 n.

Alkmaar, 83.

Allestree, William, letter from, 101 n.

Alva, duke of, 127.

Amboyna, 135.

Americas, 15.

Amsterdam:
   Admiralty, 32, 36 n., 39, 70, 104;
   Assurance, Chamber of, 17, 33-34;
   bank, exchange, 17, 24-25, 43-50, 58, 116 n., 135;
   bank, lending, 17, 44, 86;
   bourse (exchange), 17, 20, 27, 34, 47, 50, 54, 57, 74, 76, 79, 84;
   bourse, corn, 17;
   commercial capitalism, 25, 27-28, 57, 85-103;
   currency, 47-49;
   enlargement: the New Town, 18, 60;
   exchange business, 23, 29-30, 44, 52-55, 127;
   foreign capital in, 23-24, 52, 56-57;
   fortifications, 18, 60;

industry, gilds, 15-16, 24-25, 27, 61-73, 92-93;

insurance, marine, 33-35;

interest rates, 82-88;

investment of capital in the United Provinces:
   industry, 16 n., 61-73;
   land, polder enterprises, 28, 60-61;
   public loans, 74-83;
   trading companies, 28, 79-80;

investment, foreign:
   drainage schemes, 120-122;
   loans, 52, 73, 86-87, 104;
   mining and industry, 36-37, 112-115, 119;
   trading companies, 132-138;
   jewels pawned in, 107-108;

Jews in Amsterdam, 16 n., 25, 31, 58, 65, 78, 111, 116;

market, bullion, 49-53;

market, commodity, 14-15, 17, 20-23, 88-96, 118;

market, grain, 14, 21-22, 26-27;

market, munitions, 21, 35-42, 52, 64, 76, 105-108, 112-114;

organization, commercial, 75-76, 96, 140-142;

poorterschap, admissions to, 15-16, 17 n., 19, 23-25, 61 n., 62, 66;

population, 17;

port, 13, 17, 20, 60;

press, 64-67;

prices, price-lists, 20-21, 34, 54, 95-96, 118, 131;

provisioning armies, 30-31, 52;

religious toleration, 16;

revenue and credit, 17, 80-83;

shipbuilding, shipping, 13-14, 16 n., 17-20, 23, 26-27, 31-33, 40, 52, 69-70, 72, 87-88, 94 n., 105, 106 n., 111, 113;

site and communications, 13-14, 17, 127;

slave trade, 109-111;

speculative trading:

147

SELECTED ANN ARBOR PAPERBACKS

works of enduring merit

For a complete list of Ann Arbor Paperback titles write:

THE UNIVERSITY OF MICHIGAN PRESS / ANN ARBOR